D0756843

Praise for Steve Galea

Steve Galea received the Ontario Community Newspaper Association's Columnist of the Year Award for 2000 and the Humor Columnist of the Year Award for 2001. Steve Galea has been a finalist for the Canadian Magazine Foundation's Humor Columnist of the Year Award and the Canadian Community Newspaper Association's Best National Editorial Award.

"The ability to combine information and entertainment are the hallmarks of great outdoors writing. Steve Galea has quickly become one of the true masters of both. His humor column in *Ontario Out of Doors* has become a must for every reader of the magazine, myself included, and I count myself one of his biggest fans."

–Burt Myers
EDITOR/ASSOCIATE PUBLISHER
Ontario Out of Doors

Praise for Tom Goldsmith

"With his unique ability to brilliantly capture the elements of a story, Tom Goldsmith establishes himself as the premier sporting cartoonist. Frighteningly, though, the drawings seem to be based just a bit too closely on Tom's personal outdoor experiences."

–Jason Smith
MANAGING EDITOR
The Pointing Dog Journal and *The Retriever Journal*
AND EDITOR
Just Labs

MY OUTDOORS

MY OUTDOORS

STEVE GALEA

Illustrations by
TOM GOLDSMITH

Johnson Gorman Publishers

Text Copyright © 2002 Steve Galea
Illustration Copyright © 2002 Tom Goldsmith
Published in the United States in 2003

5 4 3 2 1

All rights reserved. No part of this book may be reproduced by any
means, electronic or mechanical, including photography, recording, or
any information and retrieval system, without the prior written permission
of Johnson Gorman Publishers, or in the case of photocopying or other
reprographic copying, a license from CANCOPY (Canadian Copyright
Licensing Agency), 1 Yonge Street, Suite 1900, Toronto ON M5E 1E5,
fax (416) 868-1621.

The Publishers
Johnson Gorman Publishers
2003 – 35 Avenue SW
Calgary AB Canada T2T 2E2
info@jgbooks.com
www.jgbooks.com

Credits
Edited by Robert H. Jones
Cover illustration by Tom Goldsmith
Cover design by Jamie Heneghan, Liquid Silk Design
Text design by Full Court Press
Printed and bound in Canada by Friesens for Johnson Gorman Publishers

Acknowledgments
Financial support provided by the Alberta Foundation for the Arts, a
beneficiary of the Lottery Fund of the Government of Alberta.

COMMITTED TO THE DEVELOPMENT OF CULTURE AND THE ARTS

National Library of Canada Cataloguing in Publication Data
Galea, Steve, 1962–
My outdoors: humor from the field and stream / by Steve Galea.
ISBN 0-921835-68-X
1. Hunting—Humor. 2. Fishing—Humor. 3. Outdoor life—Humor.
I. Title.
SK33.G34 2002   799'.02'07   C2002-911272-9

Author's Acknowledgments

The author expresses his appreciation to Burt Myers and John Kerr of *Ontario Out of Doors* magazine for showing me the ropes and providing me with a back page to get them tangled in. Further appreciation goes to Len Pizzey and Martha Perkins of the *Haliburton County Echo* and *Minden Times*. A humor writer couldn't ask for better places to hang his hat.

Special thanks go to the regular gang of irregulars with whom I hunt and fish. You know who you are and would, no doubt, prefer if I left it that way.

Last but not least, here's to Bob Jones for kind words, encouragement, and patient editing.

To Carol for providing a warm fire at the end of the hunt and to Ryan, Jenny, and Carmen for believing I'm the best outdoorsman there ever was, despite overwhelming evidence to the contrary.
–STEVE GALEA

To Linda, Emily, and Gordie for buying all that stuff about hunting and fishing being vital research for my work.
–TOM GOLDSMITH

CONTENTS

MY OUTDOORS

1
OUTDOOR HUMOR 101:
An Introduction of Sorts

O UTDOORSMEN, FROM AN EARLY AGE, ARE TAUGHT A MYRIAD OF essential skills. Whether it's missing Canada geese at point-blank range or putting horrific backlashes in bait-casting reels, we are given a bounty of choices and happily encouraged to pick our poison (or, if you happen to be a French angler, *poisson*). Those of us with cast iron stomachs will choose several of these dangerous concoctions, thereby institutionalizing frustration in our lives and possibly inviting a shot or two of marital discord to boot.

Despite this, every now and then a strange thing happens. Namely, we do something right in an outdoors environment. The probability of this is roughly equivalent to the chances of sneaking unnoticed across an illuminated hardwood floor while donning a blaze orange parka and snowshoes. Incredibly, though, it happens. While some might welcome this strange phenomenon, I must caution you. Essentially, it is a treacherous coincidence that leads to the unwarranted conclusion that we are, in fact, experts. And that's where the humor starts.

Of course, it's a rare outdoorsman who will just go ahead and tell others that he is an expert. Hell, who'd buy that anyway? Certainly not anyone he ever hunted or fished with, and definitely not his spouse, who's seen more empty game bags than Stevie Wonder's snipe hunting guide. The truth is, no one, not even a die-hard World Wrestling Federation fan, would fall for it. Even they are not that gullible.

So the "expert" endeavors to do what society expects of him. He either puts up or shuts up. And here's where the outdoors industry comes in. After all, he needs inspiration from somewhere. Well-meaning mentors from magazines, videos, TV, and radio, in a relentless effort to give more bang for our ten-point buck, often go above and beyond the duck call of duty. They present him with challenges that, once completed, are bound to convince even him of his own expertise. That is assuming he lives, of course.

For example, he is presented with detailed instruction on wild and esoteric pursuits such as stalking a rutting bull moose with a self-made bow. The author can do this with clear conscience because he is firm in his belief that no one other than an outdoor writer on assignment would try.

Yet later that fall, you'll catch a glimpse of our "expert" sneaking through a jungle of tag alders, slathered in cow-in-heat urine, wearing moose hide, carrying homemade bows and stone-tipped arrows. The epitome of sportsmanship to be sure, and the outdoor scribes who inspired this would be proud, too. However, only rarely will those same hook and bullet gurus deal with the genuine humor inherent in such an exciting endeavor. And, as anyone who has ever witnessed such incidents will attest, there is definitely humor here. Oh sure, it looks like pure terror on the face of it, but if you block out the ear-piercing shrieks, the rending of cloth, the broken bow, and the satiated look on the moose as he ambles off, there's often a belly laugh or two to be had.

For his part, the victimized archer tends not to speak of it for years—and then only to a trained professional at sixty-five dollars an hour. Or so I've heard.

That's a shame, too. Because not only is the "expert" missing out on the levity of the situation, but he is also now also fully qualified to add to the body of knowledge concerning the mating rituals of that large and lecherous animal. Besides that, a good hunting buddy would hear him out for about the cost of a six-pack, and hunt camp couches are far more comfortable, too.

I consider myself an outdoor humorist. Essentially, this means I can run faster through the tag alders than the archer beside me. This lends itself to the first basic rule of outdoor humor: It's only funny if it happens to the other guy. Remember this one. It's critical to your enjoyment of the outdoors.

As elementary as that sounds, it needs to be said because nobody is ever taught these things. As far as I can remember, there was never a multiple-choice question on the hunter's safety course test that dealt with witty repartee in a duck blind. But, as anyone who hunts water-fowl knows, this is really what it's all about. Ducks are purely an afterthought. Most serious duck hunters would rather miss a pair of cupping mallards than an opportunity to roll on floor of the blind, laughing at a partner who fell out of the blind swinging at those same birds.

Which leads to another basic tenet of outdoor humor enjoyment: Be prepared to run.

Here's an actual example. Little Bob and I were steelheading a river early last spring. After some discussion it was decided that we would do better at the river's mouth. Getting there entailed crossing an ice-covered feeder creek, and as Little Bob outweighs me by at least one hundred pounds and I was unsure of the ice's thickness, I naturally let him cross first. It's a good thing I did. Before he could say "Holy @!#$%!" he was touching the muddy bottom of that frigid flow and appeared to be sinking faster than the Titanic. I did the only thing an experienced woodsman could do at a time like this. "Quick, Bob" I shouted. "Throw me your wallet and car keys. No sense both of us suffering." Experienced outdoorspeople will recognize this as a masterstroke of logic. That unselfish and heroic action probably saved his life, as a desire to put a strangle hold on my scrawny throat gave him a new-found reason to live. It wasn't long before we made it to the mouth of the river, me preceding him by fifty fleeting yards. I am constantly surprised at the speed of these big guys. Yet, you will note that there are startling parallels to the moose incident described earlier.

Later, when I slipped off that icy log and ended up mounting it like a cowboy jumping down off a saloon roof onto his horse, Little Bob tried to insinuate mirth into the situation. But that, obviously, was not funny and more than anything explains why I can lip sync to the Supremes better than most. I only mention this so you will observe that it is all simply a matter of perspective.

Finally, the last important rule of outdoor humor can be summarized by: Time ages memories like a fine wine. Hell, every time I see Little Bob in the vicinity of an ice cube I can't help but chuckle. And interestingly enough, he hasn't sought help or started on that new bow yet.

What follows then are similar tales of the not-so-great outdoors. If you ask me, these are the kind that are told around hunt and fishing camps year in and year out, and remembered perhaps more than the big buck or monster fish. And that will remain a timeless truth until I acquire one of these trophies.

The point is, outdoorsmen and women love to laugh more than most. Mostly at others, but still, at least that's a start. So, read on, enjoy, and above all, spare this book if the toilet paper at that wilderness camp is in short supply. For me, at least, it was far too long in the making.

2

ROCK BASS UNLIMITED

WE WERE GATHERED BY THE BARN, NOT FAR FROM REUBEN Heycede's tractor-high manure pile. The theory being, if you're going to sit back and spread the stuff, you might as well be close enough to look over and gain inspiration—not that any of us needed more than a shovel full.

"I suppose you're all wonderin' why I called fer ya?" asked Heycede, our genial host in faded overalls.

The three of us looked to him, then longingly to the cooler of cold ones at his feet. A blistering summer sun hovered overhead, and the breeze had died down to less than a church whisper.

"Not really," said I, taking the liberty of passing the amber bottles around. "We figure you're looking to hit us up for cash. Just like always."

"I'm practically insulted," he said with an easy smile, which only told me that I hadn't tried hard enough. "Besides, my cash-borrowing days are over."

Heycede grinned like a Cheshire cat sitting at the crowded end of an aviary. "Relax, friends. Enjoy the beer."

You have to know Heycede. Him offering anyone a beer was the rural equivalent of hell freezing over. We looked at one another in disbelief, then began discussing what the underworld's hockey lineup would be like. All the while the old farmer just sat back and laughed. It was creepy.

Still, in no time flat, bottle caps were twisting like Chubby Checker, and life seemed pretty good. After all, we had just spent a fruitful morning on Loser's Lake manipulating tiny poppers and catching hefty smallmouths as well as the odd rock bass, or maybe it was the other way around. After that first beer, the details were rather unimportant anyhow.

"Ahem," said Heycede finally, as he placed one gnarly thumb under each red suspender and hoisted his pasture-pattied billy-boot up on a hay bale. Generally, when Reuben struck this sort of authoritative pose, it meant he'd been thinking. And those of us who knew the old bachelor also recognized the inherent dangers in that activity. After all, this was the guy who once believed that carrying a goose call in his front pocket would make him popular with the ladies. Like all of his harebrained schemes, this made him the talk of the town, and right after the church picnic Heycede got a fire-and-brimstone lecture from the Reverend to boot.

On the flip side, he was still seeing that cute widow lady down the line. Yes, Heycede was nothing if not crafty.

"So, Reuben, what's up?" asked Little Bob, the biggest, bravest, and most alcohol-resistant of us all.

"Well," he announced, looking benevolently toward the horizon as if to show off his sloping brow, "I've figured on startin' a conservation organization to protect rock bass, and seein' how you three is the conservin' type, I thought you'd like to be first in on it."

"Huh?" we asked, as perfectly good beer spewed out all over the parched barnyard.

"You heard me," Heycede said, smiling the classic piano-toothed smile of a snake oil vendor. "I want to protect the rock bass."

More beer was passed around as we continued laughing at the thought.

"What y'all laughing at?" he snapped. "You three catch more of them than anything else. Time to pitch in and help the resource."

"Reuben," answered Slim, "rock bass are the most plentiful thing in these parts, not counting blackflies, cottagers, and contractors, of course. What the heck do they need protecting for?"

"So they stays that way, dummy!" he retorted. "Passenger pigeons once darkened the skies, too. You guys give to Ducks Unlimited. Why not this? You take far more rock bass than ducks. I seen you all shoot."

"But DU does useful things!" Slim protested between long chugs. "They're reputable. What can you do to help rock bass? Real foundations do real work."

"That's the beauty of it. . . ." Heycede paused, then winked. "Rock bass swim in every pond and puddle of this province. We won't have to do a thing. Just maintenance work. It's a lazy man's charity."

"What kind of maintenance?" I slurred, as my rising blood alcohol level provided enough clarity of thought to sense that he was onto something big.

"Have another beer and we'll talk this over," he said. "I call it Rock Bass Unlimited—RU."

We sat around all afternoon, baking under the sun, as Heycede spoke of his vision while at the same time keeping us from parching. And I must admit, as the beer cooler got lighter and the sun got lower, the whole concept sounded better and better to all of us.

"First, we got this slogan, you see—'RU a member?' Kinda grabs you, don't it?" he asked.

By the fifth beer we were crying, happily repeating it, and high-fiving each other's foreheads.

"Then we can improve their habitat," Heycede elaborated. "You know, encourage members to skip stones into the lake and such."

"That's beautiful, man. . . ." sobbed Slim.

"They love rocks," I added, from where I lay facedown in the manger. "It's good for the little darlings. That's why they call them rock bass, see?" And that was about the last thing I remember clearly.

Late the next day, Slim, Little Bob, and I were drinking java and nursing massive headaches in the local coffee shop. Little Bob had unplugged the juke box and made it clear to everyone that head-banging music was not in order. The place was quieter than a prostate clinic after a call for volunteers.

When it came time to pay, our wallets hardly had enough to cover the cost of the creamers. Crazy Suzy snarled, slapped some straw off my head, then put the bill on our tabs.

Just then, old Reuben walked in, and to our surprise, the cheap old-timer ordered a large coffee and the fanciest crueler behind that glass. Not the usual day-old one, either. Hell, this was brand-new—perhaps the Cadillac of donuts. None of us had ever seen anyone actually buy one before.

"Hello, boys!" he snickered. "RU wants to thank you for last evening's healthy donations. You'll find a bag of habitat rocks in each of your vehicles as agreed. Take 'em out. There's rock bass to save!"

He left whistling a happy tune, and as I looked around I realized that RU already had a good start. There were three new fish at our table. Some might say suckers, but if you looked past the sunglasses, we all had red eyes.

3

WHEN PIGS FLY

WHEN I WAS A KID, THE BEST THING YOU COULD OWN WAS a nickname. If you were truly blessed, it was the kind that could easily cross over into the world of professional wrestling. This made sense, since every red-blooded boy dreamed of earning a good living by airplane-spinning opponents out of the ring.

In those days, names like Snake and Weasel were in great demand because the logic of the time suggested that even at four-foot-eleven and seventy-two pounds soaking wet, owning one of those epithets made you a shoe-in for the title. Or at the very least, it molded you into a serious contender.

Conversely, a name such as Pumpkin did not. No one could imagine a man named Pumpkin spinning anyone—outside of a dance hall, that is. And it's for this reason alone that I am a great outdoorsman rather than an internationally reviled superstar of the wrestling world.

Like most childhood rites, nicknaming had a couple of unwritten rules. First, a nickname couldn't be self-imposed, and second, some-one other than your mother had to give it to you. It was commonly understood that Gorgeous George was named by his mother. Look where it got him.

By the tender age of eleven, I was still unlabeled. Believe me, life without a nickname was a frightening proposition for a lad of those delicate years. You couldn't help but wonder when one would come. Frankly, you feared that it would originate from one of those terrible family secrets that your sister constantly yapped about to all of your buddies. That's how Pee Pee Pants Smith got his terrible appellation. Then again, with three older sisters he never stood a chance.

Still, if you were a little sharper than young Pee Pee Pants, you picked out a desirable nickname and did things to suit it. Putting the cart before the horse, if you will. Back then, I would have given my best slingshot to be named Gator. A guy couldn't help winning cage matches with a nickname like that. The facial tattoo alone would have been enough to make girls faint. Yes, I had it all planned. It's amazing just how much clarity of thought originates from the average pre-teen. In hindsight, I believe this is why lions eat their young.

With the name determined, I figured that a suitable stunt done in front of credible witnesses would seal the deal. Coincidentally, I had taken up reading during those formative years. This at the request of my teacher's yardstick and my father's well-worn vocal cords. Put that way, it all seemed reasonable enough to me.

As fate would have it, the book chosen to etch lines in my other-wise silky smooth brain was called *Modern Hunting with Indian Secrets*. Unfortunately, it was the sort of book that hardly required pic-tures. Full of useful information, that book's wonderful pages con-tained everything a boy needed to know—from snaring mice to las-soing grizzlies. I won't say that it left an impression on me, but let's just say that I still keep a lariat in the trunk. You never know. . . .

Now, the love of duck hunting is arguably a genetic defect in my family, so I read the section entitled "Trojan Horse Tactics for

Waterfowl" with more than a passing interest. It appeared convincing. Still does. Basically, it was pure native genius of the kind that gave Custer an overdone haircut. Toss a dozen pumpkins into a pond that ducks frequent, and let them get used to those orange gourds. Then, one day, you hollow one out, cut out eye holes, slip it over your head, then bob neck up with the rest of the vegetables until an unsuspecting bird swims by. Pretty simple from there on in. A quick tug and you've got duck à la orange, so to speak. Kind of slick, huh?

A farm on the edge of town possessed all of the essential ingredients to pull off this distinctly gatorlike stunt. A nice pond, a pumpkin patch, and a slew of mallards were all within sight of the nearby tree line. Thus, my pro wrestling career was practically assured.

On the following Friday night, our gang huddled in the cedars overlooking Farmer Brown's forbidden acres. Brown was a grizzled old character who had piano-key teeth and no lost love for children or trespassers, especially in October when his beloved pumpkins were ready for market. The sight of children in his tree line would invoke curses as well as rock salt and his scatter-gun. This was something Red Ass McLean knew all about firsthand. Still, that farm was the only game in town.

Over the fence we went, picking and tossing pumpkins all the way. Great splashes and cheers shattered the peaceful rural evening. Brown must have thought his pond was being strafed. He came running out, ready for action, but we were back over the wire before he ever cleared the barnyard. I still remember smiling at the sight of those pumpkins bobbing as the evening flight of mallards pitched in.

Saturday morning found me slithering under that same fence. The boys in the tree line shivered but watched with admiration as I crawled into the patch and used my dad's Buck knife to carve the headgear. Soon, I was neck-deep in the water. Parts best left dry on frigid October mornings suffered most, and I do believe that I loosened several teeth with the ensuing chattering. But pride kept me there. The fear of being nicknamed Blue Balls also provided added incentive.

Through my little slits in the gourd I scanned the frigid waters before me, impatiently waiting for those mallards to land within arm's reach of my bobbing head. Apparently, the boys had never watched a shivering pumpkin before. The sound of their laughter resonated within the gourd, and I can tell you that the acoustics were nothing short of amazing. But soon, another more terrifying sound echoed within. It was the flatulent melodies of Farmer Brown driving his pigs to the pond, which also served as their watering hole. Between a string of four-letter words, I could also hear the good farmer loading up his scatter-gun and yelling at the boys in the tree line. Feeling about as nervous as a long-tailed cat in a room full of rocking chairs, I eased over into the shallow water, the level of which rose imperceptibly as a direct result of my nervousness.

"Come over here you @%#$ pumpkin-throwing @%#$!" he screamed with total sincerity. "Old Bessie's loaded for bear. Is that you Red Ass?"

While the implications of this were playing through my thermally challenged mind, I also came to the startling discovery that pigs eat pumpkins. The one gnawing on my headgear proved the point. Naturally, something this immediate causes a person to react. In hindsight, I will concede that my actions may have been rash; nevertheless, I formulated an impromptu plan that basically consisted of springing out of the water like a startled wood duck and screeching, "AHHHHHHHH!" while charging madly for the nearest fence line.

As a side effect to this experiment in expediency, I also determined that pigs can and do fly in the face of such actions. Pee Pee Pants swore that the whole herd was fully airborne as it cleared Farmer Brown.

Regardless, by the time I ran three steps, the pumpkin shifted, leaving me with less than adequate vision. Trust me, at times like this you need adequate vision. It's true what they say about navigation in the dark. You do run in circles. And I guess with that Buck knife flailing like it was, me covered in mud, and a pumpkin sitting atop my shoulders, a simple farmer could get a bit unnerved, too.

It was then that I discovered that Brown was no simple farmer; he could shoot well even when unnerved. Needless to say, the pumpkin came off quickly, and the story ended with one quick roadrunner-like dash to the property line.

Oh, I guess I ought to mention the second rule of nicknaming. That being you can never have duplicate nicknames within the same group of guys. So, that night, as I laid in bed, I thanked God for my dear friends, Red Ass and Pee Pee Pants. . . .

4

THE MOUNT

THE GRAND DAY HAD FINALLY DAWNED, AND AS MY BROTHER and I drove to the bus station, my grin extended to about two inches behind each ear, rivaling the combined dental efforts of the entire Osmond Family. I had good reason to bare teeth. This was the day that my mount arrived. A day feared by good interior decorators and relished by those of us with more common sense, we who truly believe that the entire deer season should be declared a religious international holiday.

Once at the bus station, I went to the desk, where, without the pomp and circumstance that should have been attached to such an occasion, I smiled at the dour woman behind the counter and proclaimed loudly, "I'm here to pick up the head mount of a trophy deer. It was a big one—ten points. Shot it in Saskatchewan after five days of hard hunting. . . ."

"Name?" she asked, obviously impressed enough to recount the tale to her husband.

"Steve Galea," I answered. "It was a long shot—two hundred and fifty yards if it was a foot—and he was sneaking away when we spotted him. The wind was high and it was gonna be tricky. . . ."

"Address?" she interrupted. I suppose she wanted all the facts. I blurted out my address. Poker-faced, she said, "Sign here and go around back, Bwana."

"Anyway, wind and all, I made the shot. Dropped it right in its tracks. . . ."

"Next!" she bellowed.

It struck me that she might have been green with envy, so I cut my tale short. A few steps around the corner and I was soon the proud recipient of a large wooden crate shipped directly from the promised land: Saskatchewan. The taxidermist had kept his sacred vow. My faith in a higher being was reaffirmed. There was order in the universe.

"I suppose you are wondering what's in the box?" I asked the clerk. Curious as she was, she ambled off before I could say another word.

After loading the coffee table-sized crate into the back of my brother's pickup, we were off. Before long we pulled up into the driveway as my wife and daughter stood nervously watching from beyond the screen door. It was plain to see that they, too, were more than a little interested in the contents of my package. I had this feeling that my excitement was infectious—kind of like the Asian flu.

As curious neighbors looked on, Mart and I dragged the crate into my house, and I knew they were wondering what could be in a box that size and why it caused so much excitement. I was all for opening it on the front lawn, but the women wailed, "No!"

Some things are far too personal, I guess.

Once in the living room, we gathered around the box as the lid was gently pried off. Now to say that everyone reacted differently would be akin to saying that big government has a small credibility problem. Basically true, but not the exactly the full picture.

"EEEEK!" screamed my wife and daughter in unison.

"It's beautiful, man," said my brother.

"Just like I said," I gleamed. It was exactly as I had remembered it. Minus the huge body, of course.

I gently lifted the big ten-point head-and-shoulder whitetail mount out of the box and held it up over my head like it was the Stanley Cup. I sang praises of the taxidermist's craft, happily noting the look of blatant envy in my brother's eyes. Of course, this made it all the sweeter. My wife and daughter were uncharacteristically silent. This was the cherry on top.

"Wha. . . whe. . . where are you planning on keeping that . . . thing?" Asked my now blanching partner, a strange look of fear crossing her face. The last time I saw that look was the day when I confessed my love of broiled squirrel.

"I was thinking in the living room," I said jubilantly. "After all, it's the central room in the house. Our guests will be able to hang their hats there. It'll be there to greet everyone as they enter." I began formulating the official story in my mind.

She broke into a strange stuttering noise. It was unintelligible, but I was positive it signified an excited approval. My daughter, a sensitive soul, permitted a solitary tear down her young cheek. Happiness was my guess. My brother nodded a blessing. All the while, the sight of this magnificent trophy was tearing away at his covetous heart.

"Wha. . . wha. . . why not the laundry room?" queried my wife.

"Or how about the garage!" added my youngster. Which was unusual to say the least, for we did not have a garage.

"Calm down," I chuckled. "Since you like it that much I'll try to get us another one next year."

They both flinched.

With that I laid the large buck's head down and went to the workshop for the tools to hang it. My brother followed, all the while acting as if he was overjoyed. But I knew better. The green-eyed monster possessed him like a Wagnarian opera possessed extra chins. He was feeling the desired effect of a true trophy.

When we returned, the ladies insisted that it would look much more at home in the yard amongst the flora and fauna. I naturally rejected this claim. What would a beautiful buck be doing amidst all of my carefully placed flamingos and garden gnomes? Surely, this dramatic trophy would take away from the subtle ambience I had worked so hard to achieve. Obviously, they didn't have my flair for landscaping.

I began measuring the living room wall for dead center, an oddly appropriate term for the place where I wanted to hang a lifeless head. After marking the spot, I had my brother hold it there while my family and I looked on in silent admiration. It was a deeply emotional moment for us all. I must admit to shedding a manly tear, but it was nothing compared to the way the girls bawled. I somehow felt responsible. My chest puffed out.

There it hung, jutting out of the wall, antlers reaching across the vast expanses, dwarfing the lava lamp below it. It was all so beautiful. A Kodak moment.

Yet, somehow it wasn't right. Perhaps it clashed with the black light toreador. Perhaps not. It was something of that delicate nature, an intangible that my decorator's eye caught.

Reluctantly, I asked my brother to lower it in his aching arms. The women cried even harder, but a strange and happy smile accompanied those tender tears. It was almost like their hearts were forever touched by that fleeting beauty. But don't ask me to explain the dancing.

Now it hangs in my den, surrounded by the Elvis bust, the dime store Indian, and the other mounted critters from those wonderful hunts gone by. Each item here holds a special place in my heart, each induces a silent smile as I sit among them.

I smile at the beauty and at the memory. And, except for the visit of the odd hunting buddy to this sanctuary, I smile alone. But, oh, what a smile.

5
GUIDING MISS DAISY

IN THE SUMMERTIME, WHEN WATERS SLOW DOWN AND THE SMALL-
mouth bite is on, I love fishing small creeks. In fact, on one particular "crick" in my county, I'm what you might call a local legend. My ability to catch and release the elusive monster fish of that
tiny flow—before anyone's ever witnessed them, mind you—is practically the talk of the town. The locals can't believe my false modesty,
or anything else I say, for that matter.

With this sort of reputation, you'd think people would be dying
to procure my guiding services or at least have me provide instruction
in the fine art of telling the fish tale, but surprisingly, I get very few
bites. I'm not sure why. Once, in fact, while sitting in a bug-infested
swamp, I had time to ponder the matter as I waited for the rescue
crew to arrive. But like the county road and the creek of that fateful
expedition, the answer still eludes me.

Despite this, every now and then someone takes a leap of faith,
drinks excessively, or loses a bet, and whammo, I am back in the guiding business. With Millie, I believe it was all three.

Millie—my spouse's mother—is a country woman of the old school, with an appreciation for fish in the pan and wildflowers in the vase.

"You planning on wetting a line?" she asked as I wolfed down a second helping of her famous country breakfast.

"Yes, I am," I responded. "How'd you guess?"

"The rod, reel, vest, waders, and that stupid fishing hat were my first clues," she answered. The woman has an unerring eye for details.

She left the room shaking her head and muttering a not-so-silent prayer for her daughter. She returned with an armful of antiquated fishing gear. "Can I go with you?" she asked.

I was caught off guard. This was the first time anyone had ever asked me to take them fishing. Though I was flattered, I had doubts about her handling the rigors of the trail. It was a fair hike to the pool, and the mosquitoes and blazing sun would be constant companions. Sensitive to her feelings, I paused, then formulated the words to let her down gently. "You know, Millie," I cautioned, striking a guidelike pose, "it's a rough road I'm about to travel, and you're not exactly a spring chicken. . . ."

"You %$#&* %$#!" she clucked maternally.

That brisk exchange left me feeling very much like an Indian—there was brave talk, but I still had reservations. I mean, I was about to traverse bug-infested bogs, climb over blowdowns, scramble up and down rocky ridges, and plow through jungles of almost impenetrable underbrush for at least an hour each way. Of course, I might not get lost, but who could count on odds like that?

"I don't know," I said. "I'm seriously concerned about your safety. . . ."

"Here, I packed us a small lunch," she answered, pointing at an oversized backpack.

"Then again, no one lives forever," I reasoned.

In short order our gear was gathered, and I hefted the heavy pack. It took a bit of adjustment, some grunting and groaning and a fair bit of staggering, but in no time flat Millie stopped her complaining and wore it like a trooper. Always a gentleman, I offered to carry her Pocket Fisherman.

Soon we were trail bound, moving through meadows, hiking up hills, stepping over big blown-down trees, and weaving through underbrush thick enough to deter all but the bravest mosquitoes.

"Well, we're on the way to Old Bronzeback's lair," I said to her as we approached the bog. Which was the first time I noticed that she wasn't there. Suddenly, I was overtaken by panic. Here we were, deep in the bush, and I'd lost my mother-in-law. Who'd believe me? Never mind the fact that she was carrying lunch. Just as I was praying for a Viagra-free prison system, she called from the far side of the swamp.

Rushing through deep, leech-infested pools toward her, I sunk neck-deep only once. Fortunately, the mosquitoes pulled me out. Tattered, bit, scratched, and bruised, I finally crawled over to help Millie, who was sitting in the shade, drinking lemonade and calmly pruning a bouquet of wild daisies.

"The trail is easier," she observed, shaking her head.

After a bit of preliminary first aid, we were again moving at a good clip, and I was surprised how well the old girl moved along. I'm no lightweight to carry.

She woke me up when we reached the creek, by which time I had recovered sufficiently to wield a fly rod. We stood looking at the finest pool in the county, a big cauldron bend of flowing water that was home to Old Bronzeback, a great smallmouth that I had hooked several times. That fish weighed at least four pounds and fought like a demon. Once hooked, she'd jump, dive, shake, turn, roll, and do whatever else it took to lose you—much like the agile young ladies I pursued in my youth. Old Bronzeback was my Moby Dick, and I fully expected my last moments to be spent pinned to her side as she went under for good. With that in mind, I always managed my fly line carefully.

I'd battled her on four previous occasions, and all I had to show for those efforts was a matching set of broken leaders. Determined, I began casting Woolly Buggers to her subsurface lie behind a big boulder.

In the meantime, Miss Daisy and her Pocket Fisherman had hauled out a couple of respectable bass. Apparently, just watching my streamside demeanor was enough to tutor her in the finer points of creek fishing. I'd always heard that a good guide teaches without so much as a word. Believe me, it's true. Perhaps I should have uttered a few words on how us pros frown upon fish hogs, but it's hard to talk when your jaw hangs slack.

To Daisy's credit, after a brief tussle, she did release Old Bronzeback. Normally, I don't think I could have taken her in a fair fight, but I felt strongly about this one.

"I bet she's too tough to eat, anyway," she said. "Now quit your crying."

I managed to force a smile when she posed for the picture. Good guides will do that. But the next time she wants an expedition, we're driving to the damned Piggly Wiggly, box lunch or not.

6

CRAMADOG CRICK

IN HALIBURTON COUNTY, THE OLD BOYS WHO HUNT AND FISH love to test the limits of other folks' gullibility. Personally, I don't find this very amusing anymore. I mean, not everyone is blessed with my level of mental agility, so why take advantage of the less fortunate? No matter how few and far between.

I was saying those very words to Reuben Heycede shortly after I returned from a particularly arduous trek through another mosquito-infested bog, having once more searched in vain for his Uncle Elmer's lost mountain of pirate gold. Heycede, it seems, was crushed by my inability to recover his family inheritance yet again. But, trooper that he is, he bore that disappointment stoically, with his sad yet almost jovial belly laugh. Even in his obvious grief, he heartily supported my disdain for the torment of the naive. That's the kind of guy he is. Unfortunately, not everyone around here is like him.

In the city, they'll send a new guy for a bucket of steam. Here, they'll ask him to go to Cramadog Crick for a who-jack-da-pivey. I should know. In my time, I've sought both—and sometimes simultaneously.

Naturally, Cramadog Crick is a fictitious place and a who-jack-da-pivey is the rural equivalent of a bucket of steam. It didn't take me more than a dozen times to figure this out, and shortly thereafter Heycede said that he realized I was just bright enough to help him on his quest. Up until then, he figured I was just your average greenhorn. But after that he proudly introduced me as his Mark. Apparently, it's an endearing term that he often uses in honor of his late brother, the astronaut. I told Reuben that I was touched. He and everyone else in the barbershop couldn't help but agree.

Of course, being in this tight with the good old boys has advantages for someone who is competent with shotgun, bow, and fly rod, and it's not half bad for me, either. Heycede, for example, knows every nook and cranny in the county, and this includes several spots where black ducks land and brook trout swim, though not necessarily in that order.

The funny part about him and the other barbershop outdoors experts is that you never actually see them getting haircuts or spending time out in the bush. For the most part, they just sit there, comment on haircuts, and tell stories of huge fish and deer. When I made that observation, they said it was only further proof of their mastery of stealth. So confident was Heycede that he even guaranteed me that I'd never catch one of them out in the bush.

Of course, they must get out often—otherwise how would they know so much about the fish and wildlife around these parts? And the beauty is that they are willing to share this mountain of expertise with just about anyone who asks.

Once, they even interrupted the planning of yet another major expedition to the interior in order to draw me a secret map of the best squirrel hunting spot in the county. Apparently, they'd had their fill of Brunswick Stew.

"Best squirrel spot?" I asked, trying to maintain my veneer of coolness. All I could think of was acorns and beech trees on a high remote ridge. "Bet you it's filled with nuts, huh?" I blurted out excitedly.

"It will be, it will be," Heycede assured me.

Unfortunately, by the time I got there, the ridge in question had sunk back into the swamp from which it had emerged. And even though that five-mile walk was a blister-filled event, I was grateful for the chance to confirm such a sudden and dramatic geological event.

Shortly thereafter, the master himself offered to take me to his most secret spot. He said no one deserved it more.

While driving along an obscure little logging road, he stopped and pointed to what the untrained eye might see as an impenetrable jungle of hawthorns. After I watched a garter snake get stuck at the thicket's edge, Heycede just smiled and winked.

"What?" I asked, feeling slightly uncomfortable. Usually when Reuben gestured like that it was time to hold your breath and roll down the windows.

"Just past that mess is the best duck pond in central Ontario," he offered. "Monster bucks come to drink out of it, too. Partridge are thick in the surrounding woods, and it also happens to be teeming with five-pound brook trout."

"Really?" I asked calmly, as I instinctively dove through the truck window toward the underbrush. At times like this, I believe it's important to keep a poker face, and despite the fact that I was clotheslined by the seat belt, I did just that.

"Yes, and no one knows about it but you and me," he said.

Now, I'm not the sharpest tack in the box, but this struck me as far too suspicious. Hiding a family fortune is child's play, but good hunting and fishing spots are a different matter entirely.

But just as I was about to express my doubts by the use of a quaint little expression describing the waste by-product of a male bovine, a huge buck raced across the road headlong into the thicket.

As he crashed out of sight, ruffed grouse flushed left, right, and center. While I took this all in, flight after flight of black ducks coasted overhead, wings set in a shallow descent, and in the distance I swear you could hear the splashing of big rising trout. Even my unflappable guide seemed surprised, practically dropping the straw he held fast between his remaining molars.

On the way home, we excitedly made hunt plans while inexplicably driving through a maze of old logging roads that seemed to criss-cross, zigzag, and meander on forever. In the end I was as disoriented as a dunce farm boy who has been told to find the corner in a silo. Reuben, unobservant as he was, didn't notice any perceptible difference in my demeanor.

Later on at home, I pulled out the old topo map and realized that I didn't have a clue about the location of that piece of outdoors Nirvana. Perturbed, I dialed up Heycede and asked for his assistance in pinpointing it. Reuben was as accommodating as ever, and a mere three threats later, I had it circled in red on the map.

The next day at the barbershop, I was describing our find to some of the other boys. Heycede shot me a dirty look from across the room.

"Where is it?" asked Little Bob.

The room went silent. The clipping stopped. All eyes were upon me as I cleared my throat.

"Well . . ." I said, "just off a Y in the logging road, three miles east of Cramadog Crick."

Heycede smiled and shortly thereafter found himself a new Mark to remind him of outer spaces.

7
HUNTIN' DAWGS

I T WAS SMACK DAB IN THE MIDDLE OF GROUSE SEASON, AND THERE
I was struggling through a horrible tangle of burrs, briars, and
thorns while that putrid smell of marshy rot and wetland decay
wafted toward me. There was an ominous silence, followed by the
muffled sounds of a lightning quick movement, the kind all too
familiar to an upland gunner. Still, it's funny how a flush catches you
off guard. As I brushed through the matted coat of his dog for the last
time, Reuben Heycede emerged from his lengthy sabbatical in the
washroom, an *Ontario Out of Doors* magazine in hand, the back page
curiously missing.

"Make sure you get all them burrs out," he commanded as he
wiped the sweat from his brow.

"Brush your own mutt," I replied, as I fanned my hand in front
of my offended nostrils.

"This ain't no mutt," he snapped quickly. "He's pure bred."

"That's possible," I responded. "He certainly has a dough head."

Heycede was a hard man to insult, but this did it. That scraggly mutt was his pride and joy, and he bragged about him at every chance. "That dog put up four partridge this morning," he said proudly, placing one gnarly thumb behind each stressed-out suspender.

"Yes, but only because they were roosting in that tree he decided to mark," I said. These subtle points were somehow forgotten by the grizzled old upland gunner. Besides, Heycede got one bird out of that deal, and to him results counted.

"That dog has got style, huh? You don't think Elwood Dunsford's pretty little dog can put you onto birds while standing on three legs do you?" He said this proudly, as an incomplete and malformed smile emerged from under three days growth of beard.

"Uh, no," I admitted. "Definitely not."

Heycede bought the dog in the early summer, possibly in an attempt to divert his own fleas, but primarily to shut up Elwood Dunsford once and for all. Dunsford, the accountant who lived down the concession line, was a man who liked what Reuben considered the finer things in life. Things like food, sleep, and shelter.

"He's a city-bred sissy!" Reuben once announced. "That's what he is." You must bear in mind, of course, that to Heycede there were only two kinds of city folk: sissies and weirdoes.

Dunsford, formerly of Toronto, actually qualified as both since he now lived the life of a country gentleman—fly fishing in the spring and summer, and hunting over pointing dogs in the fall. In keeping with this admirable lifestyle, he spent considerable money on a fine English setter with the pompous name of Forever Traveling Europe. She was the snootiest dog any of us had ever seen but, boy, did she get us birds. It was Elwood's claim to fame, and Heycede couldn't abide anyone stealing his thunder. Up until then, no one could find birds like him.

After only one season of hearing the boys sing loud praises about Dunsford's dog, Heycede finally blew the dust off his notoriously tight wallet and bought the mutt that was now happily humping his leg.

"He's affectionate, too," he pointed out, moving away uneasily.

In an effort to outdo the elegant name of Forever Traveling Europe, Reuben called his dog Always in Continent, a name I thought a fitting tribute to the way it hunted.

"Forget Europe—there's no place better than North America," the old farmer proclaimed at the barnyard coming-out party. Naturally, we all drank to that. Most of us drank beer, but Elwood Dunsford, who smoked a pipe and sipped some sort of expensive ice wine, merely snickered.

"Reuben," Elwood asked as he straightened out his tweed sports jacket, "what breed of dog is that, anyway?"

"Uh . . . it's a new one," Heycede replied. "They call it a thicket-marking flusher. Yeah, that's it—they are all the rage in and around Sault St. Marie."

"Oh, come on Reuben," countered Elwood. "Enough of the lies. It's a mutt."

"Ain't a mutt," said Heycede, as he hastily rolled up his sleeves and spit on his knuckles. "It's a purebred. Paid nearly twenty bucks for it, I tell ya."

The rest of us scattered, cleared a space, and began collecting the pitchforks and beer bottles.

"Forever Traveling Europe is a purebred," Elwood said hesitantly, noting the precautions and slowly backing away. "He's pedigreed."

"Well, I clipped my dog's toes last week, too," Heycede responded smugly. He looked at us and nodded curtly.

At this point, Little Bob had the foresight to whisk the pencil-necked accountant away. But the damage was done.

A week later, Dunsford, Heycede, Slim, Little Bob, and I gathered for a ruffed grouse hunt along the old trail where partridge were thick in the black growth to the sides. Although apologies had been made and this was billed as a conciliatory outing, everyone knew it for what it was: a showdown between Heycede and Dunsford. The winner would rule the local coverts. Either way, grouse hunting around our county would never be the same. The odds were heavily on Dunsford, and I almost felt sorry for my old buddy.

Soon the kid shooting gloves came off. Dunsford was reluctant to have his pedigreed dog sharing the spotlight with the likes of Always in Continent, and the normally polite accountant made no bones about it.

"Does your mutt know what he's supposed to do?" Dunsford asked Heycede as he prepared to unkennel Forever.

"Oh, he knows what to do, all right," Reuben responded calmly.

Soon enough the dogs were released. First was Traveler, who ranged close by with tiny bells ringing as she glided competently through the thickets in search of grouse. She worked like a well-oiled machine: efficient, single-minded, and tireless. Dunsford was justifiably proud.

Heycede, who now looked worried, whispered to his dog and unleashed the brute. The big dog, which sported a shiny new cow bell, ran straight for the thicket that Traveler was working, then a horrible ruckus ensued as bells clanged and grouse flew out from every side. While Slim and Little Bob dropped a bird each, Heycede and Dunsford ran toward the briars.

Dunsford rocketed out of the impenetrable part screaming, "Oh my god! Get a bucket!" while in midstride to the creek. As the frantic accountant returned with a Orvis hat full of cold creek water, Heycede calmly emerged from the foliage smiling.

"Young love," he announced happily.

The hunt ended soon after the nuptials, and Heycede's Always in Continent came out on top, so to speak. That mutt ruled our underbrush for the rest of the season, and Reuben was never happier.

Dunsford was rarely seen after that. Some say that he hunted distant habitat with his dog and that a few months later he quietly gave away a litter of scraggly bastard pups that had the curious habit of going on point while standing on three legs.

8

THE TROUBLE WITH NYMPHS

I T DOESN'T TAKE A GENIUS TO REALIZE THAT A CROWDED HOSPITAL room isn't the best location for a relaxed and pleasant conversation. This is especially true when the participants are hardcore fly fishermen, and the only flowing water around can be heard collecting in the next patient's bedpan. Even so, I felt the need to try. After all, my concussed friend Leonard needed this civility more than a brook trout needs cold water and mayflies. This fact was made entirely apparent by his shaky hands and that nervous, uncharacteristic, doe-caught-in-the-headlights look in his eyes.

Leonard's well-ordered world had collapsed. His formerly gentle new bride went ballistic and left him, coincidentally just after his unexpecting cranium said hello to the nonstick side of a frying pan. Worse still, he missed two fly fishing club meetings and perhaps the best hatch of the year. And it was only Wednesday. The rest of his week promised to be just as bleak.

"How are you feeling, buddy?" I asked, believing this to be a safe place to start. Like all fly fishermen, I felt uneasy about opening a can of worms.

"My head's still throbbing," he replied, addressing the IV pole three feet to my left. "But at least my vision is almost back to normal."

"You'll be tying size 28 gnats in no time," I smiled, making sure our eyes never met. Which wasn't exactly difficult, considering the way his were wandering independently around their respective eye sockets like two trout jockeying for the best feeding lane.

It was a merciful lie. Aside from his recently rearranged outlook on life, his hands shook like an electric toothbrush being held by a frightened Chihuahua. In his condition, Lenny, a formerly brilliant fly tier, would be lucky to thread an 8x leader through a basketball hoop. This pained me. Who was I going to get my midges from this year?

"It happened so . . . suddenly. . . ." he began cautiously.

"Do you really wanna talk about it?" I asked reluctantly.

"I guess . . . what I remember most . . . um . . . is the frying pan. . . ." he stammered.

"The river?" I said, hoping that he was changing to a more pleasant topic, for he loved to fish the Frying Pan River.

"No, not the river," he growled. "That big Teflon one we got as a wedding present. She swung it so fast. . . ."

"Katie seemed so nice, Len. Why?" I asked hesitantly, not really wanting to pry into any dark family secrets.

"I don't know. Really, I don't. She's normally very quiet and timid."

So is a Bengal tiger, I thought as he proceeded.

"I recall being on the phone. She was in the next room, the kitchen, cooking. That was just before the bloodcurdling screech and the charge."

I listened intently as he told his morbid tale of fly tying and marital woe.

"I wasn't doing anything to provoke this," he said. "Just speaking to Little Bob from the fly fishing club about fly tying night. I remember keeping it to a whisper because I didn't want to get her all worked up. It coincided with her plans—she wanted to go shopping for frilly drapes and bath soaps on that very same night." He shivered. "Can you imagine?"

I nodded in utter disbelief. Was she mad?

"Still, that was no reason to do this. . . ." he motioned feebly to his bandaged head.

"What did Little Bob want?" I asked, trying to steer the conversation into less dangerous pools.

"Nothing in particular, but I let him know that I got a new vise." He beamed momentarily, then frowned. "I remember her ears perking up at that, but it didn't matter—I was gonna tell her anyhow. It didn't seem like a big deal."

"Honesty is the best policy," I lied in a most convincing manner.

"Little Bob talked about the new skein of Phentex wool that he wanted to acquire from his wife Thelma's knitting basket, so naturally I commented on that."

"What'd you say?"

"I merely mentioned that it sounded real nice, and I wouldn't hesitate to tell Thelma that I'd really like to tear off a piece, too."

The thought of good fly tying material seemed to cheer him up.

"Me, too!" I added. "I saw it. It's phenomenal stuff."

"It was at that point I heard the first low growl." He shuddered, remembering where he was.

"Women do that all the time," I assured him, having no qualms about sharing my vast store of marital wit and wisdom. Most times I can't give it away. "It's instinctive. Probably even hormonal."

"Anyway, Little Bob mentioned that we were going to tie some stonefly patterns at the next club meeting. So I told him I'd love to tie one on. He asked me if I was sure, since, as you know, I am a confirmed dry fly man. But I told him loud and clear that I hadn't made a nymph since before I was married, and I was certain I wouldn't mind making one or two now. . . . I guess I got a little excited there 'cause I'm sure she heard me, but still . . ." He paused, his brow furrowing. "It was then that she picked up the frying pan. I didn't pay it no mind. Thought she was going to cook with it. Boy, was I ever wrong."

"Who'd have thought differently?" I added softly, as his story slowly fermented in my mind.

He adjusted his bandage and continued unloading. "Then Bob starts telling me about a new fishing satchel he's got. He bragged about all the fancy features and how it straps on like a fanny pack. Says I should buy one. But I said I had a great old bag and she serves me just fine."

I acknowledged the old canvas bag that he'd carried on stream for as far back as I could recall. Functional, yes; pretty, no.

"But you know him. He pushed it. Like it was the best thing since tapered leaders."

"He's like that," I concurred.

"So, just to shut him up I conceded that I'd replace the old bag soon—and with a newer, prettier model."

We looked at each other through a silent pause as the fog suddenly lifted.

"You didn't see it coming, did you?" I asked.

"No, sir. She was quicker than a steelhead's first good run. I believe she's watched entirely too much Xena."

I left for a moment as Len made a hurried long distance call to his mother-in-law's distant lair. When I returned a few minutes later with two coffees, he was attempting to smile.

"Is it all cleared up?" I asked.

"Yes, I believe it is," he grinned. "She's going out to buy a new frying pan and everything."

When I left my buddy, he was in far better spirits. So upon my departure, I said I'd call him next week before the club's tribute to Woolly Buggers. He thought about it briefly, then begged me to spare him the favor.

9

SHOOTIN' THE BULL

IT WAS AN EARLY SUMMER MORNING MANY YEARS AGO, AND THIS young man's fancy had turned to love. In those god-awful days I watched the world through rose-colored glasses. This, of course, was stupid since I had twenty-twenty vision. Suffering from this tomfoolery, not for the first time, but definitely for the worst time, I did uncharacteristically witless things. Some of those deeds still haunt me, especially the ones performed in full view of my hunting buddies. Things like missing the odd hunt to be with her. Ugh! Even worse, once I tried to teach her how to shoot. I remember it all like a train wreck. . . .

She and I walked hand in hand to the old sandpit. Her carrying a bag of empty pop cans, I a .22 rifle and a large number of rounds. We looked like a highly militant litter patrol.

When we arrived at the prescribed range, we smiled lovingly at each other and gave each other a quick kiss. Then, in the spirit of partnership and equality that was supposed to guide us for the rest of our days, we neatly set up ten pop cans for the lesson. It seemed so pure and simple.

A word to the young fellows here. Don't do it! Sweet God above, if you ever get to feeling the way I did that day, run fast and run far. I mean, I have missed hunts. Ugh! In hindsight, I believe hypnosis and sleep deprivation had something to do with it. Now to get on with this morbid tale. . . .

We paced back twenty steps. I looked deeply into her eyes and said, "Here we are. By the time we're done, you might be able to shoot nearly as well as me. But don't be disappointed if not. It's taken years to hone my marksmanship."

She looked at me longingly and replied, "Shoot as well as you? No. . . ."

"Yes," I insisted.

"No. . . ." she cooed, bosoms heaving.

"Yes," I repeated, slightly distracted.

"Oh, go on!" she replied.

There was my one chance and I blew it.

This important and memorable conversation went on endlessly. Thirteen years later, just before she packed her bags for good, she looked back to this type of banter and said the words every married man fears: "How come we don't talk like we used to?"

I answered, perhaps incorrectly, "Because my brain grew back."

A multiple choice calculus question would have been far easier. Yet there we were on that lovely summer's day years ago, with ten cans to the front, a rifle at our feet, and bluebirds still soaring o'erhead. I showed her how to load the .22, gave a quick dissertation on shooting, then went over the basic safety rule. "Always treat the gun as if it were loaded, and never point it at anything you don't want to shoot." I spoke in a low and intense growl, and my nostrils probably flared. I had a hairline back then, too. She never really stood a chance. I then asserted, "I sighted in the scope yesterday. I didn't want to waste your time."

Then came the misunderstanding of the century. "You're the most considerate man I've ever met," she remarked.

I took that to mean that she hadn't got out much. After that, I didn't give it much more than a passing thought. I was hoping to hurry this thing up so I could drop her off at her mom's while I went on a fishing weekend with the guys. I quickly demonstrated the fundamentals of shooting, then squeezed the trigger and spun a pop can. I looked at her and smiled.

"You nicked that one!" she squealed. I had impressed the hell out of her. Little did she know that I wasn't aiming at that one. Why spoil it?

I began to coach her. "Now it's not as easy as I made it look. Breathe slowly. Take your time and don't be—"

I was interrupted by the crack of a shot. A pop can flew violently upward, spinning like a gymnast launched out of a cannon. Lucky shot, of course. I smiled uneasily, knowing this.

She quickly reloaded and repeated the process, four more times in lightning succession. My jaw dropped. She was jubilant. Little did I know this was to be a familiar pattern for the next few years.

With four cans of frightened Pepsi still gleaming in the hot summer sun, she said, "I hit most of them dead center, but that last shot was off. I think I hit the *S*. Was that okay?" She blurted all this out in one quick statement.

"Uh, yeah," I said, beginning to unload the gun.

"Let's shoot some more," urged young Annie Oakley. "It's fun and there's probably so much more that I can learn from you. Can you shoot skeet with this thing?"

I shuddered at the thought. Back then it all seemed so harmless, and I was so naive. Now, those old tricks wouldn't work. I went to the target and kicked aside all of the cans. I dug into my pocket and pulled out my lucky quarter, one that had been with me since boyhood, and not just because I was cheap, either. It had seen it all. I was certain that coin could not be destroyed by man. And it turns out I was right.

I found a piece of driftwood and wedged the charmed coin in a crack of the branch, then placed it against the backstop. I walked away knowing that this tiny target would bring her down a notch or two.

"Cans are easy. That silver caribou over there is a bit harder." I smirked, went prone, and took careful aim, almost hoping not to hit. The crack of the shot was quickly followed by an explosion of dirt a scant inch from the shiny object. I was happy. It was close enough to prove my point. I stood up and handed her the rifle.

She took a careless offhand stance and pointed down range. The end of the barrel shook like a blender full of ball-bearings. No chance, I thought. I laughed quietly while she yanked on the trigger and obliterated the quarter.

"The scope must have been knocked out of whack," I snapped quickly.

"Huh?"

"Well it's obvious, isn't it. Didn't you see me miss that coin? I never miss. Why I remember the time Martin and I were shooting bumblebees for sport—I only took head shots at the drakes! And never from closer than forty good paces. We'd bark them off sunflowers. That's not all—"

"You're right," she interrupted, putting her trigger finger to my lips.

"Huh?"

"You're a much better shot than me, and we both know it," she admitted.

With that settled, we left hand in hand. Not long afterward, impressed by her impeccable honesty and sound judgment, I proposed.

10
Two Misses and a Mister

THERE WE WERE ON THE SECOND LAST DAY OF THE SHOTGUN season for deer, and things looked bleak. In fact, a vegetable tray at an anti-hunting rally faced better prospects. Then again, it probably had a higher combined IQ level to work with.

Our group of four had hunted hard, and we were still lacking in the bragging rights department. This was an unusual situation, I might add, and one that I generally wouldn't mention except for the fact that it further illustrates the magnitude of the blunders that I feel it is my painful duty to relay—year after year. Naturally, since the mishaps weren't perpetrated by me, the word *painful* might be a slight exaggeration. With that in mind, let's get on with this story.

The boys of the Tall Tales and Short Shots Hunting and Conservation Society were gathered in Reuben Heycede's barn once more. The occasion was not a particularly auspicious one. One of our foursome had missed—yet again.

For the sake of this story, we'll call him Little Bob, which happens to be his real name. Anyway, Bob's head was hung in great shame, as befitted someone who had just missed the buck of a lifetime at kiss-blowing distance. When we arrived at the scene shortly thereafter to shake Bob's hand and mutter insincere things about what a good hunter he was, we found him despondent. Like all good hunting buddies, we were overjoyed. There was no deer to dress and drag out.

The tracks in the snow told a grim tale. Apparently, the big fellow had missed the buck as it posed broadside at five yards and smiled at him. Once again Old Victory, as this forest monarch was named, had eluded an injection of lead, a permanent place on Little Bob's wall, and a family barbecue or two. I believe this is because he is destined to be mine (and yes, I'll admit that taken out of context, this would sound weird).

In any event, at that juncture in time, I would have rather had oral surgery performed on me by a farsighted grizzly bear with the shakes, than be Bob. It was bad enough that he was feeling so low at this joyous time of year, but to have your buddies turn mean on you was the icing on the cake. Unfortunately, hunt camps can be like that. One little miss and you become the camp goat.

In any case, there he stood, shaking his head and rubbing the seat of his hunting pants. Although the latter was a customary pose for him, this time he was doing it to ease the sting of the three sets of hunting boots that had just left imprints there. This was the physical penalty for a miss in our camp (negative reinforcement, if you will) and the reason why so many of us wore our hot-seat cushions inside our coveralls.

"I can't believe I missed Old Victory," he moaned. He was suffering emotionally. It was pathetic, and I was sure glad it was Bob rather than me. Then again, I would have never admitted it was the big buck that I'd missed. I would have spent hours arguing that it was merely an anorexic fawn with big feet that I was trying to scare off. In my opinion, integrity is highly overrated.

"Yes, Bob, you missed," I chortled gleefully. "At five yards, no less."

"We forgot to practice at that range," added Slim in a horrible below-the-belt shot.

"You should have let him come a little closer," advised Reuben.

Then we laughed like a pack of hyenas circling a hamstrung zebra. It was all in good fun, of course, with the added bonus of burning far less calories than if we had actually dragged out a real big buck.

Yet Little Bob, who had suffered the slings and arrows of one thousand misfortunes, was particularly distraught by these remarks about his marksmanship. It's not like he never used his shotgun. We all shot skeet religiously in the spring and summer, and we were duck hunting fanatics until the deer season began. Then we practiced seriously with slugs and buckshot. None of us would think twice about folding a crossing teal, although folding the laundry was certainly a different matter.

So we were hard pressed to explain his missing a standing, big-antlered giant at spitting distance. After debating all of the options, only one explanation would suffice: buck fever, the most dreaded of all outdoors afflictions. The horrific fever wasn't unknown around those parts, but it was never easily proven, either. Most of us would rather admit to being lousy shots than confess that Bambi rattled our nerves. Still, there were subtle ways of uncovering the truth.

"Check his temperature!" cried Heycede, as he frantically waved a rectal thermometer. As scientific as this was, it even scared me. It's sort of the last thing you want to see in a hunt camp.

"No need," said Slim quietly, and the rest of us breathed a little easier. "His knees are still trembling. It's a definite case of the fever."

"Those shaking knees are probably still from the doe this morning," I added, trying to bolster Bob's self-assurance. "The five-yarder was simply a case of mistaken trajectories. I imagine that he estimated the range was eight yards and shot high!" We all cackled like heavily laden hens.

Now the fact that Bob missed Old Victory at five yards was certainly damning, but earlier that morning he had also missed a large, fleet-footed doe at what he reported to be sixty yards. Of course, as any deer hunter knows, that meant thirty real yards.

The big fellow's confidence was obviously shaken, and he was just recovering from that miss when he encountered Old Victory. That rendezvous put him over the edge. He was walking in circles, muttering something about going postal at a petting zoo and then taking up golf. The rest of us, kindhearted as we were, offered to buy the clubs.

And on it went. Somewhere during the ribbing, poor Little Bob earned the nickname Two Misses and suffered the degradation and humiliation that only true friends can provide. He endured it well, with an admirable dignity and a slightly quivering lower lip. We were able to relax on the suicide watch after only three days.

Later, when his emotional wounds had scabbed over, Bob approached me in privacy. He was obviously seeking consolation from my renowned sagacity. Still, I kept an escape route in mind.

"Why me?" he murmured sorrowfully. His head was still hung appropriately low, and though we each handle grief in our own way, I thought the black armband was a bit much.

"Bob," I replied sympathetically, "deer hunting is like that. First there's the thrill of Old Victory and then there's the agony of doe feet. . . ."

As I chuckled, the big fellow walked off, groaning just like Old Victory after those missed shots.

11
WORMS

ACK WHEN WE WERE KIDS, LONG BEFORE WE DISCOVERED FLY rods, spinning gear, BB guns, and girls, there were worms. Admittedly, those were simpler times. Then again, we were simpler as well. This fact was in accordance to what dads, teachers, and the natural laws of the universe have always maintained.

As a young lad of seven or eight, I was endlessly fascinated and delighted by worms. Much like the girls of my youth, they were slimy and gross to the touch. The difference, though, was that a fellow could impale worms on fishhooks without fear of being forced to kiss and make up. But even so, a kid could at least hold his head up high after smooching with a night crawler. With this in mind, worms were our preferred choice of friends.

For a while this was fine. But suddenly and without warning, a strange thing happened. The girls in the neighborhood started to look as good as the worms. We were only seven or eight, mind you, so they didn't look better—not by a long shot. But somehow girls had transformed from Barbie-toting, house-playing, cootie-carrying monsters into creatures on par with fat, juicy, night crawlers. Back then this was a minor miracle. Naturally, we resisted this phenomenon with every bath-avoiding, slime-loving, sunfish-catching bone in our scrawny, mud-caked bodies. And it was this simple act of defiance that provided the balance needed in our pint-sized universe.

Yet, a funny feeling would come over you as one of those pony-tailed terrors pranced by and stuck out her tongue. It's very much like the feeling I still get when I eye a really fine shotgun. But as I said, we withstood their charms. Which is where the worms enter into this tale.

In those pre-computer game days, summertimes were spent doing one of three things: chasing girls, catching fish, or providing our mothers with new laundering challenges. Needless to say, each of these activities required worms. The real pros (and I don't mean to brag) could do all three simultaneously.

It was on one such occasion that I learned a valuable lesson—one of the few in my life that had little to do with hunting or fishing, even though I was catching panfish all through the tutelage.

There I was sitting on the dock, minding my own business. Which on that day consisted of watching a red and white bobber and setting the hook every time it went under. Combined with this high stress activity was a study in spit trajectory and stone skipping. School never really ended for a guy like me.

Suddenly, from out of nowhere, trouble appeared in pigtails and a pink bathing suit. Her name was Juliet, and as she approached, my bladder went weak.

"What ya doing?" she asked demurely.

"Fishing," I replied. "What are you, blind?" Which I thought was an obvious sort of answer since I held a fishing rod in my hands and was proudly doing battle with a monster perch.

"Oh, I'm gonna swim here," announced fair Juliet, apparently unimpressed by the heroic struggle. "Okay?"

"You are not!" I said, putting the hapless fish on my stringer.

"I am so," she said very plainly and much to my annoyance. With

that determined, she quickly laid down her Snoopy towel and, without anyone even telling her to do so, meticulously ironed out all of the wrinkles with her clean hands. Talk about sick. Then she dipped her toe into the water in that dainty way which I could never fully comprehend but which I hoped would attract a good muskie or at least a hungry snapping turtle. Yet I sensed impending defeat. Any minute, her toe would give her the okay, and she'd go in, scaring away all of my fish.

Relishing my desperation in a way that only girls could, she dawdled and twirled her delicate fingers in her cute sun-bleached hair. For my part, I tried to show no fear.

"Go away, goofball!" I yelled in the diplomatic fashion of the time.

"Make me, you Neanderthal," she challenged, although I'm still at a loss to explain why she chose that moment to compliment me.

From there on in, I remember events in bits and pieces. The worm. The window-shattering shriek. The ninety-mile-an-hour pursuit. It was the one pearl in an all-too-small necklace of childhood victories. Anything seemed possible that day—even the muskie.

But somewhere between the slapping of the worm across her perfumed head and the scruff-of-the-neck hindrance provided by my father, I contracted a bad case of puppy love. In retrospect, it wasn't so strange. Her screams could shatter ice in a duck pond, and she ran like a white-tailed doe. What more could a young outdoorsman want in a girl?

And so, later that day, after Dad released me on my own recognizance, I returned to the place of our encounter and waited for her. I held a gift in hand and an off-key song in my pint-sized heart. I clutched Ernie—my best rubber worm. He was totally lifelike and a small token of this smitten boy's affection.

Juliet soon walked down the trail picking brown-eyed Susans, her facial tick still as I had left it.

"Hello," I said bashfully as I dropped ten feet from the limb overhead, Errol Flynn style.

She stopped cold, her tick redoubled, and her skin color drained to alabaster.

I wanted so dearly to impress her, and even though I had obviously made a fine start, my mouth went dry, my heart pounded fiercely, and my bladder was making me do a lively little two-step. She stood there, frozen in her tracks like a moose in the headlights. Don't think I didn't find this endearing.

Her immobility gave me reason to believe that it was time to act decisively. So I did the only thing that entered my lovesick mind. I raised the plastic worm and lowered it slowly into my open mouth as I had done a hundred times before. It was a trick that never failed to impress my street hockey pals.

That was the last I saw of Juliet. But I do remember the cloud of dust and her sensual greenish tinge. She broke my heart, but, as I said, she taught me a valuable lesson. That was the last time I ever stopped fishing to wait with baited breath for a girl.

12
THE BACKPACK

I**N THE MIDST OF A RECENT MOVE, THE LIKES OF WHICH RIVALED** Moses' flight from the Egyptians, I came across my trusty old frame backpack. Just dusting it off rekindled mixed emotions— back spasms as well as fond memories—about times when all of my worldly possessions, and several I had surreptitiously borrowed from my father, fit inside its myriad pockets and compartments.

Bright orange and labeled with a large Canadian flag, that backpack was one of the first pieces of outdoor equipment I ever purchased, right up there with fishing rod, tackle box, slingshot, BB gun, entrenching tool, and matching toilet paper holder.

I suppose I was merely a product of my times. Every outdoors magazine of the day ran a cover photo of a strong, young outdoorsman striking off into the wilderness with gritted teeth, camouflaged clothing, and an overloaded, fluorescent backpack. In his hand was a compound bow or a fly rod, and three steps behind him was a buxom and adoring young woman clad only in Daisy Duke shorts, a tied-off shirt and hiking boots.

As a red-blooded teen-ager, I envied that fellow. My lustful eyes appraised that photo; I would have given almost anything to spend a week in the wilderness caressing that bow. It was state of the art.

At the time it seemed like a reasonable idea. Then again, so did disco. Any idiot, me included, knew that an outdoorsman had to be mobile to find good hunting and fishing. And you had to carry your gear in something. The Charlie Brown lunch box of younger years simply wouldn't cut it, if only because the Snoopy thermos took up too much space.

But with proper packing techniques, your typical twenty dollar backpack could contain a Volkswagen Beetle and several of its occupants. Stuffing that pack to the brim was not only an art form, it was a prerequisite to being an outdoorsman. No self-respecting youth would be burdened by anything less than a spine-compressing pack bulging dangerously at the seams. You never knew, after all, when the need for self-sufficiency might kick in. Like I said, these were the teen-aged years.

On a typical outing, you'd carry a case of beans, several dozen wieners, fourteen gallons of water, kindling (in case there was a shortage of it in the surrounding woods), three Buck knives, a Bowie knife, a hatchet, Swede saw, fishing rod, gun, ammo, decoys, tent, sleeping bag, tarp, full-sized Coleman stove, naphtha, mess kit, canteen, three changes of clothes, toilet paper, entrenching tool, and a solitary match. Canoe and paddles would sometimes be strapped on top. And after ripping apart the whole mess, you'd discover that the can opener was left at home.

This kit would suffice for a morning's jaunt in the wilderness. Overnighters required weightlifting belts and special trusses. Loaded up, the wilderness exploring outdoorsman sort of looked like the Beverly Hillbillies' car without the tires.

Of course, there was no such thing as a typical outing. Every hike into the backcountry was special, in perhaps the same way that my teachers used to assert that I was special on parent–teacher interview nights. You never knew what to expect out there, so you planned accordingly—without a clue.

These days outdoor travelers are spoiled, what with Global Positioning Systems, all terrain vehicles, lightweight gear, and advanced search and rescue techniques. Sure, there are still a few of us who can get into trouble despite all of this, but it was much easier back when you had to navigate by the sun and stars. Of course, back then those celestial bodies weren't nearly as advanced as they are today. Which meant nine times out of ten you'd get very happily lost. Once again proving the wisdom of purchasing a backpack.

Empty, the pack weighed less than the tail feather of a hummingbird. The salesman said so, and back then they didn't lie. To a seasoned outdoorsman a pack's weight was important because unless you had a string of mules or a two-headed coin and a friend who always called tails, you'd have to carry it, too. That's where many a trip ended.

Fully loaded, these things were heavy. At jump-off points to the wilderness, it wasn't uncommon to see whole groups of young hunters and anglers lying on their backs like capsized turtles, victims of overloaded backpacks. Some say that these spinning backpackers were the first break dancers, but I'd like to remember them with a little more respect.

But I digress. The bottom line was that if you had help getting under the shoulder straps, or if your father owned a swing-boom crane, you were ready to meet anything that the great outdoors had to offer. That is as long as it didn't require a can opener or more than one match, of course.

I remember one hike vividly. Red Ass McLean and I were searching for the source of the mysterious and predominantly urban Rouge River just east of Toronto. My father, knowing nothing of adventure except how to fabricate an ad hoc swing-boom crane, happily offered to drive us there as long as we promised to stay for a day or two.

Red Ass and I settled on a spot a few miles away from the alleged headwaters, then stepped into the vast wilderness of the Rouge River valley. Back then, the world was a gentler place, and unsuspecting adults thought nothing of giving thirteen-year-old boys machetes and

naphtha. Being cognizant of newly emerging environmental issues, we used them sparingly to gently hack and burn a trail through flora and whatever slow-moving fauna we could catch.

It was an arduous task to blaze a trail through riverbank thickets while carrying a backpack loaded with enough weight to counterbalance Orson Welles on a seesaw. Taking the adjacent paved bicycle trail would have been easier but a far sight less glamorous. After eight hours of trail blazing, we stopped to make camp. Red Ass and I smiled. This was the kind of mobility young outdoorsmen strived for. Yet, even though we had traversed a great expanse of wilderness, by some miragelike effect, we could still see the road.

We never did find the source of that mysterious river, but that's no fault of those backpacks. In fact, it was more to do with a strange shifting of the sun and currents that we found ourselves overlooking that mighty river's mouth at Lake Ontario.

Yet the trip was not devoid of discovery. For instance, I finally ascertained the true meaning of slipped discs, a term I had previously attributed to faulty brakes. I also discovered the urge to travel light for the next little while, allowing that twenty-five years qualifies as a little while. Maybe it had something to do with simplifying my outdoors experience, but at the tender age of thirteen, when it came to lengthy walk-in expeditions to wilderness settings, I guess you could say that, more than anything, my aching back packed it in.

13

A Boy and His Duck

WE HAD GATHERED ONCE MORE FOR OUR ANNUAL WEEK OF cards, old jokes, tall tales, and the shooting of the odd duck or two. The excitement of old friends congregating, the anticipation of the next morning's hunt, and the fierce race to the washroom after the long drive up are things I will always recall. But more than those, I remember the day they took Buford.

Buford was a decoy. Not just any decoy, mind you. Buford was my lucky decoy. My secret weapon, a wooden block carved into the likeness of a bufflehead drake. Majestic and sleek, black and white, cool under fire—that was Buford. You would have liked him.

With Buford in the dekes I had never been skunked. Buford brought me good fortune. Even though he was a diver duck, he had that sexy charm that hen mallards found irresistible. Drakes liked him, too. He was a duck's duck. Carved him myself. That wooden bird and I were a team. We were more than that. My wife said we were as close as any two inanimate objects could be. Between you and me, I think she was jealous.

By my description thus far you may have got the idea that I was somewhat attached to the bird. I'll admit I was, but it's not like I talked to it . . . much.

Naturally, this kind of rapport with a block of cedar wasn't widely approved of in our hunt camp, either. I wasn't blind. So it didn't surprise me when Buford went missing just after our arrival. It was an annual thing.

"Which one of you idiots has Buford?" I asked diplomatically.

There was silence in the ranks as they tried to figure out who was being addressed.

"Very funny, guys. We've all had a good laugh now, but he's sick and he needs his medication," I lied.

"He's a decoy, Steve," said Dan, the brightest of the group. Apparently, he saw through my little ploy. If it wasn't for him it might have worked.

"He's probably run off with some cheap plastic mallard," said Ron, snickering.

I lost it and lunged at him, arms flailing like a windmill gone mad. Fortunately for him, Zoom, Mart, Dan, and David held me back. Otherwise he might have hurt his beefy knuckles on my face. But he deserved it. Buford only dated wood and that dope knew it.

After they untied me, someone suggested that I should sleep and maybe Buford would show up unharmed in the morning. Being emotionally crippled, I took that advice. A solitary tear rolled down my cheek as I glanced at the spot on my pillow where he usually sat. At duck camp, we had never been apart. Sleep came in restless fits.

The camp awoke before the sun rose, and we each got dressed and prepared our gear for the hunt. I was anxious but kept my cool. The fact that I put my pants on backward might have betrayed some distress, however.

David kindly ended the suspense. "Look!" he said, pointing to the kitchen floor. "There's the little trollop."

There was Buford, all right. His bill was smeared in cheap fluorescent lipstick. A burning cigarette was taped to his lower

mandible, and he was clad in a flimsy, low-cut pink teddy. Surrounding him were three plastic drake mallards in bow ties, a pink lawn flamingo, and several horny-looking garden gnomes. I said a silent prayer, thankful that the guys never got weird on me.

We all had a good laugh. But deep in my heart I knew that the camouflaged Gore-Tex gauntlet had been thrown down squarely at my waders. It was now a matter of duck camp honor. I had two options: revenge or the ancient Japanese suicide ritual of *seppuku*. Luckily, my ceremonial swords were at home.

That morning I hunted with Zoom, the wise old patriarch of the camp. He was my mentor, the man who taught me from age fourteen how to hunt. More than that, he had over forty years of hunt camp experience. Nobody could make a greasier egg or stink up the outhouse half as well. He was wise beyond his ears, which were legendary. He would have answers. So I waited until we were alone in the blind.

"Honorable elder," I said, "Buford has been violated. My honor is at stake." (What I actually said simply can't be put here in print.)

"Better that twelve high-flying Canada geese empty their colons on your hunting hat than to suffer a waterfowler's disrespect." (Again, I cannot accurately reproduce his two-word answer.)

"Who could have done this?" I asked. But to be honest, the whole situation reminded me of flatulence in a duck blind—there's is no denying it, and everybody knows who did it.

"Seek those who shoot three quick shots without pumping," he hinted.

So, just as I suspected, it was all of them. Ron, Dan, David, and even Martin (Buford's godfather), all shot autoloaders. Each of them was too lazy to pump. Seeing red, I devised a scheme.

That morning went well for all of us. Buford again performed magnificently, and a few birds fell as well. I must say that more birds decoyed after we removed the pink teddy, though.

At midmorning breakfast the conversation turned to that poor innocent wooden bufflehead.

"How is Buford today?" asked David, grinning.

I looked down to where the decoy sat in my lap. "He did just fine. Last night, nothing happened you know."

"It sure looked that way," declared Dan. Everyone laughed but me. I would do that later. The talk turned to the birds taken and the hits and misses of the hunt.

After breakfast and with the dishes done, we all sat down to clean our shotguns. The auto boys all sat at the table, sharing the same cleaning kit and discussing the merits of their weapon over a pump gun. They all glanced at my trusty Browning pump shotgun and Zoom's ancient Ithaca Featherlight and joked about tennis elbow.

Alone in the corner, I stewed. Of course, everyone in a duck camp stews. It has a lot to do with the diet. Not much time had passed before each of the boys staked out a couch or recliner and took to napping. Everyone, that is, but me. I had work to do. . . .

Later that afternoon Zoom and I were together again in the marsh. Mallards and wood ducks were plentiful and decoying well. The four others were in nearby blinds, each three hundred yards or so distant. But when the shooting started, an odd thing transpired. Zoom commented upon it first.

"Something strange is happening with those boys, Steve."

"Whatever do you mean?" I asked, openly smirking.

"Well, every time a flock passes them, they're only putting out one shot each from those fancy autos. And, if you listen real hard, I think I hear the Lord's name being misused in various creative ways." He then looked to me and smiled a knowing smile.

"Well," I stated flatly, "those things are kind of sensitive, not like our pumps. You know, I heard they only work as single shots without those little rubber O-rings."

"Don't suppose that they forgot to put them back in, do you?" he queried.

"Doubtful," I responded, then glanced over toward Buford.

Zoom, noting this, did likewise. "That decoy's got something around its neck," he observed.

I smiled and Buford seemed content as well. And why not? He looked good wearing his new rubber necklace.

14
LAST DANCE OF THE HERON

THE HERON WAS A MISERABLE, MYSTERIOUS OLD MAN WITH A large beak who, like his namesake, stalked the rivers alone. As I get older and my nose gets bigger, I have come to understand that this in itself isn't such a bad thing. Hey, when I take the time to smell the roses now, I get full value.

But the Heron had no sense of humor, which was inexcusable to a boy who thought the Holy Trinity referred to Curly, Larry, and Moe. In any case, the Heron was the first fly fisherman I had ever encountered, and for this reason alone, I found him funny. There was method to his every cast and a plan for every drift. To him, fishing seemed to be an intellectual exercise—something totally foreign to me. With him and the bird he resembled motion was never wasted. Herons don't dance.

I would watch him from a distance, as you would a great blue catching frogs in the shallows. Get any closer and he'd curse or take flight after you. The difference, I suppose, was that he didn't squawk and drop a load on takeoff. Then again, he wore chest waders, so you couldn't be certain. The smell of his old gear did nothing to convince me either way; in fact, my money said those waders were full.

In spite of this, the old fellow fished with a fine cane fly rod and hung streamers skillfully in the current, whereas everyone else I knew hung worms in the trees for the most part. His were nice streamers, too. Gray Ghosts and Supervisors expertly tied.

He did this even though a plain black Woolly Bugger or a juicy old worm pulled from a back pocket would have done just as well on those aggressive, fly-destroying, smallmouth bass that we sought. The Heron fished with great style if not good nature.

I didn't know the word *curmudgeon* back then, but in hindsight, this described him as perfectly as any other word that I'm permitted to put in print. He never acknowledged junior anglers with so much as a nod. His efforts were directed solely to the fish, the currents, and maintaining his bad temper. When he retrieved his beloved streamers, the rest of the world was on hold. I respected him for that, but I also thought him a bit of a snob. There were few fisherman on that stream, so there was room for professional courtesy. Even if some of us did drift a red and white bobber over a piece of lead and a garden-fresh dew worm.

Once, hoping beyond all hope that his yappy bark was worse than his very substantial overbite, I approached and greeted him at Three Rock Pool.

"Nice day, Mr. Heron," I stuttered. In hindsight this casual approach might not have helped.

He responded with the only two-word phrase I couldn't find in the family dictionary, though, God knows, I tried. Even when spelled with a "Ph", it was missing. This, more than anything, made me realize that he wasn't exactly a creekside Art Linkletter. His throwing rocks at me, though, was the real clincher.

The Heron fished a pool selfishly, as if it were his. He'd not share it, especially with a worm-dunking boy, no matter how humble, good looking, intelligent, or astute. Talk about arrogant. Realizing this, I steered clear, mainly because I was taught to respect my elders. So I gave the gruff old fart his space and prayed religiously that he'd keel over by next season.

That summer, though, he became my nemesis. He was my worst nightmare, someone with a car who had as much free time as me to fish the creeks. He had no parental restrictions, either—he always got there earlier and left later. He ruled the best pools like a five-pound pike in an aquarium full of goldfish. And his teeth weren't that much better either.

I asked about him at the barbershop where I had once watched him sit sullenly. Even the good-natured barber, Guiseppe, said he went through life wearing a face that resembled "de hugly hend ova horse." Something, he complained, that was hard to offset with a four-dollar haircut.

"Budda he's blind as a batta, an' he hayta kids anna snakes," said my hair-cutting pal with a knowing wink.

After that, whenever our paths crossed, as people's do on small rivers and trips to the outhouse, I was neither rude nor friendly. And the Heron could have cared less. But in my mind, he had to go.

The river we fished was like a dream date: beautiful, open to suggestion, uncomplicated, and cheap. The smallmouths there loved a well-presented bait, and if they wouldn't oblige, the rock bass would. There was never a dull moment. Still, the big bass were as rare as teeth in a hockey player's mouth. A three-pounder was a local trophy. There was one hanging in Guiseppe's barbershop. Back then I weighed about seventy pounds, so it seemed significantly larger. To this boy, three-pounders were the stuff of dreams.

One fateful day late in the summer, I sat on a bluff overlooking Three Rock Pool, feeling smug. I had just discovered that bronzebacks love crayfish. Below me, and unaware of it, the Heron materialized. His rhythmic casting of streamers made for a good show, even though I prayed that he'd snag a skunk on a back cast.

That day the water was alive, and his line tightened time and again, pulsing with the strength of a fighting fish, shedding water, spray glistening, making rainbows in the summer sunlight. At the end of each lively battle, he landed a big creek smallmouth. And with the release of each, the Heron danced. It was a silly little jig that telegraphed ripples, mostly from his third chin, and it divested the flabby old curmudgeon of all dignity. I liked him a bit more for that, and though I felt like a streamside voyeur, I continued watching.

It's rare to see another angler at work when he's unaffected by your presence. Here's where you learn secrets. There's no pretense, no holding back or showing off. You might just as likely see the angler pick his nose as his fly. A Woolly Booger, if he combined the two. It would make for great television. "Smile! You're on *Candid Angler.*" Something like that.

Although it was entertaining for a while, I wanted in on the action but knew he wouldn't share willingly. To him, I was an immature young pup still wet behind the ears. I scoffed at that, finished my lollipop, and got up. After all, he was catching genuine three-pounders.

As I began my walk to the water, his beady eyes intercepted me, and he told me to scram. I went upstream for a moment and then reappeared. There was enough room for the both of us, and I meant to fish the run.

For a quiet old guy, he sure knew a lot of unflattering adjectives, many of which proved useful in later life. I rigged up and ignored him, just as he did everyone else. Unconvinced that imitation was the sincerest form of flattery, he stopped fishing and waded across the chute, intent, as he quaintly put it, on "ripping off my arm and sticking the wet end in my ear."

It was then that the first of several water snakes drifted down and got hung up in his net. A first, I imagine for this creek.

"Sn. . . sn. . . snake!" he screamed in a high-pitched voice that must have been reserved for special moments such as this.

By the time the snake dislodged itself from the mesh, the Heron had cleared the bank and was halfway up the bluff. The commentary never stopped as he hightailed it into the sunset. Those wader legs rubbed so frantically together with each long stride that the smell of smoke and burning rubber hung heavy in the air. It gave his Red Ball waders new meaning, I'm sure.

I stood there at the pool, grinning from ear to ear. I was alone with the bass and a fancy box of streamers that I added to my tackle box. The next day, at the barbershop, I told Guiseppe tales of three-pounders—some of them even true. Then I went to the toy shop, replenished my stock of rubber snakes, and learned to dance.

15

WING SHOTS

RECENTLY, A HUGE FLOCK OF MALLARDS REMINDED ME THAT I'm no slouch when it comes to wing shooting. While modesty prevented me from publicizing this before, I believe that the cat is now out of the bag, what with so many people acknowledging that I'm a wing nut and all. They are right, of course. I am a great wing shot—it's the head and body that I miss. This is fine, since I love waterfowling, but I can live without the prerequisite accompaniments of plucking, cleaning, and getting cold water shaken on me by a wet, overworked retriever. Because of my wing-shooting skill, I'm happy to say that, lately, I've not been bothered much by any of these nuisances.

Although not hitting a duck sounds relatively easy, anyone new to duck hunting needs to understand that missing a flock of thirty tightly packed birds with a salvo of three wide-open patterns of several hundred pellets each isn't as simple as I make it look. Sure, almost anyone could do it once, perhaps even twice, but it takes the timing of Gerald Ford chewing gum on a Stairmaster and the gun-handling skills of an orangutan to be consistent.

But that's no reason to despair. Let me stress that I didn't learn how to expertly miss a duck in just one season, and neither will you. Even now, if I fire enough shells, sooner or later, one's going to come down accidentally. After twenty-five years of hunting, I am not ashamed to say that this still happens on occasion.

Like anything worthwhile, success comes only with patience and practice, but the rewards are great. Learn to miss and you'll have more time to enjoy a hot toddy in camp while the rest of the boys are out in the cold autumn sleet pulling pinfeathers. The best part is, they'll share with you, anyhow. After all, since time began, that's been the hunter's way.

So how do you cash in on this eccentricity? Well, experience tells me to avoid any circumstance that places shot string and duck within the same time–space continuum. Barring this, the bird will continue toward Acapulco, albeit with a cleared colon and jump-started heart. But the real trick lies in missing cleanly, while convincing your buddies that you are merely incompetent rather than purely lazy. This takes a bit of finesse. I'm proud to say that Zoom, my favorite uncle and mentor, pioneered these strategies. Back when other farsighted hunters were just beginning to see the merits of empty bag limits, Zoom was the guy you'd always see in a hunt camp photo who didn't hold a single feather. In fact, his early retrievers hardly knew what a duck was.

Hunting with Zoom is a pleasure. When he shoots, he's intense. He swears, rants, rages, and often throws his shotgun far into the marsh. But that's only rarely, like when he hits a bird. Most times, his inaccuracy is nothing short of amazing!

It has taken dedication and hard work, but Zoom hasn't cleaned a duck since that fateful day in 1963, when he swears that high winds

and a stray pellet let him down. Yet, being the consummate pro, even then he faked an illness in the middle of plucking and never finished the job. Considering the vastness of his skill, he's amazingly humble about it all.

Like all greats he has learned from his mistakes. First off, he's never bought that bargain-basement brand of shot shells since. "You need a quality shell," he advises. "Forget the cheap stuff—one stray pellet can ruin years of hard work. You want a shell that gives consistent, tight, accurate patterns. That way, with practice, you can work around it."

He is also a stickler who dedicates himself to practice, steadfastly honing his shooting skills at least every second or third season. "The thing is not to overdo it," he insists. "That's a rookie's mistake. A new duck hunter figures that just because he missed one hundred straight clay birds he knows what he's doing. Next thing you know, he hits one, and his confidence level plummets. It's hard to shake the memory of a solid hit, and that's no good. Missing is psychological. Your mind has to stay out of the zone."

His advice on hunting is just as poignant. "A full choke is the only way to go," he once whispered, while we were drinking hot toddies in the cabin and marveling at our dry retrievers.

"Because of the denser pattern?" I asked.

"Not gun choke, idiot. I mean *the* full choke. Like when the geese are coming in and you get up too soon, act real nervous, and pop off three quick shots without touching a feather. It helps if you can get your knees to shake, too. That's a full choke!"

"And a modified choke?" I asked.

"That's what happens when your hunting buddy gets hold of you."

"What about a lead?"

"Well, that's fine if you can run," he said, "but my knees are worn out from shaking. . . ."

It was only then that I realized I was in the presence of true genius. Perhaps I can best illustrate how it all comes together by recounting our last hunt.

Zoom and I drew the short straw for blinds. We were set up by a beaver pond, where a multitude of ducks literally had to fly down a narrow creek bed to park in the decoys. The situation looked grim. Missing would be difficult if not impossible.

Suddenly, a couple of wood ducks announced their intentions and coasted in. When they were on us, Zoom yelled, "Now!"

After the smoke cleared, six empty shells lay in the blind and one drake woody floated belly up.

Zoom eyed me and shook his head.

"Couldn't help it," I said sheepishly. "They were cupped and way too close."

That afternoon he humbled me. Time and time again, birds would come in, practically floating stationary over the decoys, and, miraculously, after each pass, the birds on his side would take off unharmed.

My retriever and I were not so lucky. By day's end, I had a limit, even after shooting from the hip on the last three. Chin down and despondent, I carried the weight of those birds back to the cabin.

As I sat plucking birds with the rest of the guys, the old master came out to the porch, pipe in mouth, hot toddy in hand.

He sidled up to me and smiled. "Don't worry. We all have bad days. You made one nice shot on that crossing mallard. Never touched a feather."

"What's your secret? One eye open or both?" I asked, referring to that age-old shotgunning question.

"Neither." He winked.

I smiled. The ducks have been safe ever since. . . .

16
LANDMARKS

PICTURE, IF YOU WILL, THREE YOUNG RABBIT HUNTERS gathered somewhere in a quiet hardwood valley. Chickadees flit happily from tree to tree. Snow covers the woodlands in a picturesque scene of northern beauty. It is late January. The temperature is low enough to cause serious reproductive damage to a brass monkey. Regardless, nature calls—to all of us at once. Soon three distinctive and truly artistic works in saffron are displayed along the snowbank—not the kind you'd ever see on a Christmas card but unique in their own way.

"Time to get back," I stated nonchalantly, looking across that desolate valley.

"Yeah, I promised the wife I'd be home for dinner," said Joe, better known as the Happy Wanderer. He was staring, in that vacant way of his, far up the vale.

"At least you didn't promise you'd bring home dinner," added my brother Martin, as he gazed down the draw.

We had hunted snowshoe hares all morning, and as usual, it was

Bugs over Elmers. There were plenty of tracks to see while wandering in a ragged, haphazard line through the bush. I even got off a shot or two. But, being the conservationist that I am, I deliberately missed. I do this kind of trick shooting quite often. Sometimes I have been known to use colorful language after a particularly good miss, but that's just to draw attention to my great skill. I'm nothing if not a showman.

My two companions missed quite a few as well. But they weren't trying to miss like I was—they're just really bad shots. Hey, it's my story, and I'll tell it any way I want.

So here we were in this unfamiliar valley. At least to my brother and me. The Happy Wanderer had been here before, and that's what scared me. The Wanderer is an old friend, and as the name implies, he gets around. Joe is one of those guys who swears he never gets lost in the bush. The fact of the matter is that his sense of direction is as true as a *National Inquirer* headline. Even knowing this, for some inexplicable reason, we usually let him be our guide.

We all took one last, longing glance at the winter wonderland around us, and then we headed home—in three different directions. After a few steps, we all looked back. It was time for a huddle.

"The truck's up the draw away over there," said Martin. Pointing to a stand of the most common trees in these woods, he smiled smugly and added, "I remember those poplars."

"No, I've been here before," Joe responded. "We go that way!" But the way he said it revealed that our guide was having that old sinking feeling. His quivering lower lip was a dead giveaway.

I threw in my two cent's worth. "It's that way about five hundred yards." I had no clue either, but being the man that I am, I surely wouldn't admit to it.

"Look," said the Wanderer," I've hunted here a few times, and that means I've got seniority. Not only that, but I actually remember this place. And besides, we're going back to my truck. A man knows where his truck is."

We faltered under the pressing weight of this irrefutable logic. A word or two followed from my brother, neither one complimentary. It was getting cold, the wind had picked up, and nasal passages dripped like a garage sale faucet. You get the picture—no further adjectives are needed.

"Why don't we just backtrack?" suggested the one bright star in this desolate galaxy. Like I said, it's my story.

There was agreement. Go figure. We picked up Martin's tracks in the heavy wet snow and began to retrace them. All was good. Then we came to a point where we had crossed our own prints in pursuit of the wily wabbit. Several times. The forest floor had more footprints than an Arthur Murray dance school diagram. A web of tracks led to this area. It was dilemma time.

After the ensuing lively debate, we picked a likely path. Of course, each of us chose a different likely path, so we were back to square one. Meanwhile, the brass monkeys were suffering.

"We obviously came from up that slope," Martin remarked flatly.

"Not a chance," said I, disagreeing just for the hell of it. "We came from our mommy and daddy."

"Shut up!" they cried in stereo.

I smirked, knowing that I had succeeded in uniting our merry band. They now knew that time in the bush meant time with me and my stupid jokes. They were motivated, so I knew we'd be home for dinner. Subtle leadership has always been my trademark.

Joe and Martin quickly concurred on a route—away from me. I dawdled behind with the chickadees. They seemed to be laughing at this unfolding comedy of errors. The fact that this thought had also crossed my mind made me very nervous, so I rejoined the boys.

About an hour passed, by which time the brass monkeys were now eunuchs. I was having serious doubts as to my future fertility as well. Being an optimist, I came to the conclusion that things would eventually thaw out. But still, I thought about new uses for my mittens.

Then we happened on a familiar setting. A snowbank with a trio of yellow portraits. Full circle. This advanced geometrical concept hadn't occurred to the Wanderer yet.

"We must be near the road now," said Joe, confirming my theory that there was not even a tenuous genetic link to Albert Einstein.

My brother and I watched each other's jaw drop.

"Explain," was the delayed response.

"Well, isn't it obvious?"

"Huh?" we asked brightly in unison.

"If we aren't near the road, then why is this yellow snow here. Do you think three guys walked half a mile from the road just to take a leak here?" Joe wore a smug yet dull-eyed look.

Martin and I stood silently while Joe's brain started to defrost. Suddenly, it happened. He stared at the ammonia art.

"Oh, so you think those are the ones we did, huh?" The rebuttal was indignant. He was rapidly approaching hysteria.

"No, I believe that three Keebler Elves urinated on this very spot in order to lead us away from the cookie factory," I said. With that I reached into my pocket and produced a compass, something I never leave home without. I took a quick bearing and pointed to the west, where the road was.

In the ten minutes it took to get to the vehicle, Joe spoke of my mother in a very impolite manner. Martin shook his head and mumbled something about adoption. But the chickadees and I—well, we just chuckled.

17
SHADES OF THE PAST

LATELY, TO THE WORLD'S GREAT LOSS, I HAVEN'T GIVEN MUCH counsel on the subject of fishing. Mostly, I suppose, because people aren't as gullible as they used to be. You can thank our politicians and the advertising industry for this sorry state of affairs. It's no wonder our civilization is on the decline.

I mean, when a short angler can't pawn off a tall tale or three, something is surely rotten in Denmark. Unfortunately, you couldn't even say it was the monster pike you caught on your last visit there. No one would believe you. It's almost enough to make a person take up golf. Almost.

There was a time, away back when people were honest, when you could tell your closest fishing buddy that you caught a limit of monster walleye on cherry-flavored jujubes, and there'd be a better than even chance of him believing you. Oh sure, he'd snicker and act like he didn't, but the next time you were out fishing together, you'd see a top compartment in his tackle box filled with a melted gooey mass of them. Of course, in all fairness, you'd be loaded down with the lemon

Life Savers he swore by, and he'd see them and laugh like the hyena that you always maintained he was.

These days, as I said, things are sadly different. Anglers are more educated and fairly literate. Some are even skeptical, believe it or not. This does not provide fertile ground for good yarn spinning, and it's certainly harder to pretend to be an expert. With this in mind, I've subscribed to Abraham Lincoln's adage, "Better to remain silent and appear a fool than to speak loudly and remove all doubt." Still, actions speak louder than words, so on most days, I'm euchred no matter what I do.

Regardless, last opening day for steelhead, I was compelled to offer advice to the scrawny, pimple-faced youngster on the far bank, when he cast a heavy spinner into the bush beside me. I watched in horror as he reefed back on the lure, which broke free from its death grip on the flora and quickly acquired the velocity necessary to slay an angry cape buffalo, perhaps even a rogue mother-in-law. The lure buzzed like a super-caffeinated hummingbird, barely missing his unprotected eyes before safely coming to a hollow-sounding thunk of a stop.

Minutes later, as he slowly arose from the long grass and attempted to dislodge the deeply embedded spinner from his greasy forehead, he looked around and grinned sheepishly in that idiotic way mastered only by teen-aged boys and fools caught red-handed in the ladies room. Veteran that I am, I grimaced, horrified at the carnage, knowing full well it would take a good half-hour of fishing time to re-hone that treble hook and realign the bent spinner shaft.

"You know, perhaps a pair of quality fishing glasses might be in order," I lectured, as I coolly emerged into the light from the shaded section of the creek. "It's all fun and games until someone loses an eye."

I pointed to my own fishing glasses, the polarizing effects of which somehow seemed diminished in the high noonday sun.

Noticing me for the first time, the impaled lad ceased his dramatic soliloquy on the pros and cons of body piercing and smirked as

teen-age boys with fishing lures lodged firmly in their heads are apt to do. I may be nearly forty, but I haven't forgotten what that's like.

"Yeah, right." He laughed, as he headed upstream, the lure's Colorado blade still spinning strongly in the wind.

I felt good giving that advice, though I realized that it hadn't sunk in any farther than his No. 2 Mepps. And, although I thought his hysterical laughter was odd, he'd just been beaned squarely in the forehead by a bullet-sized hunk of metal. Somehow, it all rekindled fond memories of my youth, particularly of my father and his sage advice on fishing.

"Son," I remember Dad saying during those frequent half-hour father–son chats, "maybe you ought to take up the piano."

"But Dad, I like to fish," I'd insist, while rubbing the fresh Band-Aid on my forehead. He'd shake his head, mumble something about a death wish, and continue sharpening and realigning my spinners, never quite understanding my attraction to overgrown creeks and whitewater.

Once, out of respect and while nursing a splitting headache, I did give up fishing for a short time to take up carpentry. Of course, this meant working in Dad's workshop with all of the neatly arranged tools that were his pride and joy. Never before or since have I seen him this emotional. There were genuine tears in his eyes as he watched me work my magic in his only sanctuary. He returned a few minutes later saying that I belonged amidst the worms and fish, and in his most gentle act of fatherly love, he presented me with fishing glasses, a small mirror, and a hook disgorger, then hurried me out of his workshop.

Back then, fishing optics were still in their infancy. Selection was limited to units that looked better suited to arc-welding or riot control. In retrospect, I couldn't blame him if the glasses he presented me had "dweeb" written all over them. Then, he was only slightly older than I am now, so how could he know any better?

Despite the dweeb factor, I wore them once on a fishing trip with the boys. But during that ordeal, I endured more wisecracks than

King Solomon's outhouse, so I retired them until Halloween, when I dressed up as Roy Orbison.

After that I'd sport them only when fishing solo. I mean, sure, they were uncool, but they revealed a whole new world to me. Suddenly, I could make out fish on the bottom, and if it wasn't for those glasses, I'd still believe that the springy snag in Three Rock Pool was an immovable smallmouth named Larry the Lunker. Besides, these were my formative years of fly casting, and no one, least of all me, was safe.

Well, times have changed. The glasses I wore on that day with the Colorado-kid have protected and enlightened me on many outings. When combined with a fishing vest, hat, and neoprene waders tight enough to excite an Elvis fan, they also enhanced my natural sense of cool. At least I thought so.

To me, this was evident as I worked my way up and down the trout stream that day. Every fisherman that I ran into commented on my eyewear. There must have been fifty who noticed. "Nice glasses," they'd say, as they chuckled or steered clear in wide-eyed wonder. Presumably, Young Metalhead had preceded me. Knowingly, I giggled, too. The young fool was probably happily fishing, not realizing how silly he must have looked. I smiled, remembering the awkwardness of youth, noting that with age comes knowledge. And knowledge is cool, even if accompanied by a spare tire, flatulence, and irreparable hair loss.

When the day had ended, I sat in my car, ready for the ride home. After adjusting the rearview mirror, I saw myself wearing a cool pair of fishing glasses minus one lens, which had somehow fallen out and escaped my notice. I looked like Ray Charles' half-brother. Suddenly, I laughed, shook my head, and realized it was just like always. Even after all these years, I wasn't half as cool as I thought.

18
MAKING TIME FLY

THE DAY WAS PASSING AS SLOWLY AS AN OLD, TWO-LEGGED turtle strolling straight uphill through a muddied field of molasses-covered broken glass. Get the picture? Sundays at duck camp can be like this.

Hell, if it wasn't for the time-honored pastimes of cheating at cards, setting hotfoots, placing whoopie cushions, and lengthy dissertations on a buddy's poor hunting skills and character flaws, a guy might have nothing constructive to do at all. It would have been a whole lot worse if we hadn't matured so much in the last few years.

Despite this new-found maturity, there's still a certain danger when you place six full-grown men in a tiny cabin that only has one washroom—especially after chili night. Yet this is the price most hunters will pay for a chance to spend quality time together in and around the great outdoors.

Unfortunately, though, this was the Sabbath Day. In the part of Ontario where we were hunting, the discharge of firearms other than bows is prohibited on Sunday. Naturally, this gives waterfowl a decided advantage when riding a tail wind at thirty-five yards. In other words, to us, it was a day of rest, but the natives were restless. Perhaps this explains why we had already deliberated noisily on the normal politically incorrect discussions. By this I refer to the regular hunt camp stuff—the merits of union vs. nonunion, politics, religion, decoy setups, the best shotgun chokes, the most effective waterfowl loads, the greatest hunting dogs, the sexiest women of all time, tom-*ai*-to or tom-*ah*-to, just to name just a few of the more important issues we tackled. And, surprisingly, although there was no agreement on any topic, no one was seriously hurt, either. After all, these were the same debates, year in and out. There were no surprises. Sundays at hunt camp are nothing if not absolutely routine.

Finally, though, we did come up with one ultimate universal pet peeve, the only miraculous thing that we could all agree on. That being the irrationality of the lawmaker who had deemed Sunday, in our neck of the marsh, a nonhunting day. Each time a fresh flight of worry-free waterfowl flew by the dock, a new and unflattering adjective was added to this anonymous politician's rapidly expanding title. Generally, though, he or she was deservedly known as the Stupid $#@*! Moron. Needless to say, the Stupid $#@*! Moron would get no votes from the occupants of our cabin, let alone a chance to kiss our babies. Big Ron, in fact, pointed out the only thing that he'd allow to be kissed by such a person, and, believe me, it wasn't pretty.

Meanwhile, houseflies, like the waterfowl wearing party hats and enjoying a day of rest in the nearby marsh, were becoming plentiful and annoying. As a result, the card game in progress was regularly interrupted by the sharp slapping sound of a fly-swatter communing with an insect. Being acutely aware and sensitive to the anti-hunters' view on this issue, we only hit them hard enough to buckle their knees and then only in self-defense. Still, it wasn't long after the first of many swatter-induced deep knee bends that our powerful hunting instincts, up until then held in check, escaped and focussed on this activity. In the time it takes for a tired hound to close its eyes, each of us had a flyswatter of some sort, as well as a new and genuinely fool-

ish grin. Politicians be damned. Fly season was open! A hunter, after all, must hunt. And besides, how big could the fines be?

We took after the flies with the gusto of those who love the wing-shooting sports. An added bonus lay in the fact that we had a huntable population and bag limits that were more than generous. And, believe it or not, with these primitive weapons, hunting was even kind of sporty. Especially when taking flies on the wing.

Now, I'm not saying that the boys in our hunt camp are competitive. Hell, someone else already beat me to it. But soon things were getting just a little crazy. I believe it was Martin and Ron who set up the first permanent blind utilizing the Nachos bag and salsa bowl. And I'm also reasonably certain that it was Dan and Dave who gathered up all of the dead insects, buckled knees and everything, and set them up as decoys, in a nice J-formation, facing into the wind. A strong wind, incidentally, caused by Martin, Ron, and the Nachos and salsa. Calling, I'll admit, was my idea. A typical hunt sounded something like this: "Buzz! Buzz! Bzzzzzzzz . . . Bzzz . . . Bzzzzzzz!"

"Don't overcall, you idiot! They see the dekes!"

"Stay still. One's circling!"

"Hen or drake?"

"Er . . . never mind. Take 'em!"

SMACK! SMACK! SMACK!

"#$%@! Why did you do that?"

"He landed on your forehead. Honest."

SMACK!

So the sound of swats, cursing, whimpering, and laughter filled the air, just like a real duck hunt. Flies dropped, well, like flies, I suppose. Which isn't a pretty picture, but it does do nicely to illustrate the point. We were hunting in earnest. In no time it was evident that Danny, who crouched in the "flyway" between the kitchen and washroom, had the best spot. Even though it was pass shooting, he was getting enviable action.

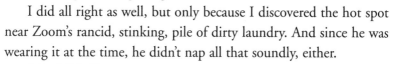

I did all right as well, but only because I discovered the hot spot near Zoom's rancid, stinking, pile of dirty laundry. And since he was wearing it at the time, he didn't nap all that soundly, either.

"Ouch!" he'd say.

"Hold still or you'll ruin the hunt," I'd respond. But did he listen? No. . . .

As in all forms of hunting, it wasn't long before the game figured out that it was dangerous to be in the area while hunters were about. Soon the flies got sophisticated, skittish, and even decoy shy. They even tore themselves away from Zoom. Being experienced hunters, we quickly modified our tactics and took to jump shooting. Personally, though, I thought it was ridiculous when Mart and Ron tried to bring in the canoe. So did Zoom, who drove them out of the cabin with a broken hockey stick and some original and colorful language. For some reason, he was what I'd characterize as cranky. Knowing his unpredictable nature, I quickly decided to find more agreeable hunting grounds.

By midafternoon, the novelty, like the flies, had worn thin. Worse still, Dan now resumed his role as the camp cook and insisted that we clean and eat what we had harvested, just like we did for everything else that we hunted. We all laughed, knowing he was joking. After all, no matter how it felt, this wasn't really hunting, was it? Still, at dinner, not one of us touched the peppercorns in the stew.

19
SNAP SHOTS

NOT LONG AGO, MY BUDDY THE WANDERER AND I FLIPPED through his photo album of hunts gone by. This is something we do whenever we feel at risk of accidentally telling a hunting story truthfully. Quite often, a quick look at those pictures is all that's needed to remind us of the official versions of the stories that we flog each year at hunt camp. I guess you could say that it keeps us dishonest in an honest sort of way.

Like it or not, you also learn things about your pals in these jagged romps down memory lane. To my surprise, this was the case that particular day. It happened as I scrutinized a blurred and dog-eared photograph that lay loose just inside the cover of the album. Although difficult for the lay person to discern, I instantly recognized the Wanderer, younger, to be certain, and with a fuller head of hair. There he stood with lines of fear still etched on his face. Beside him was a newly killed cape buffalo. That great and dangerous beast still wore a malicious grin that was truly scary, even in death. To me, that photo captured the moment and said volumes about why a man hunts. By some miracle, my friend had stopped half a ton of brute force with one well-placed shot.

"I never knew you went on safari," I said with quiet respect as I held up the old photo.

With that dull look that he possesses in spades, he looked to me and then examined the image. "What are you talking about?" he asked. "Hey! That's my mother-in-law posing with a circus chimp. Karen was wondering where that picture had disappeared to."

Squinting, I gave it a closer look and, I must say, to this day I remain unconvinced.

This just shows what a brilliant hunt camp photographer the Wanderer really is. His photo collection has more decapitated heads than the French Revolution on a good day. If you can't recognize the hunter in a photo from the chin down, you're probably out of luck. Add to this a flair for poor composition and a serious lack of focus, and you have all the hallmarks of great hunting photography. Joe's hazy images could be anyone, provided they have at least one chin, three days growth of beard, and a camouflage or blaze orange jacket. Is it any wonder I didn't recognize his mother-in-law? Who among us would?

Then again, that's what brilliant hunt camp photography is supposed to do. The fuzzy, unidentifiable objects in these sorts of pictures lend themselves to spontaneous tale telling, a pastime that the Wanderer and I have lowered to a high art form. As an example, I once told an entire grouse-hunting saga based on a shadowy Polaroid of a dog sniffing a dried-out pasture patty. For all the world, he appeared to be staunchly on point if your imagination was vivid enough. One of my buddies, engrossed in the tale, even passed comment that it was a "nice mature cock grouse in the red phase."

Later, I used that same photo to insinuate that my dog had rescued me from a grizzly bear. Of course, you don't get photos like that often.

I'll admit I am not the greatest outdoor photographer in the world, but with my old camera I very nearly was. Unfortunately, that is history now. My wife traded it in as part of a deal to buy me a new auto focus model. She meant well. Really.

"Only an idiot could mess up with this camera," the salesman advised her.

Despite that sweeping assurance, my photos suddenly went from unrecognizable kaleidoscopes of earth tones and shadows to focussed, centered shots of me posing beside undersized bucks or unfortunate birds that had happened to fly behind the one I was actually aiming at. It almost ruined storytelling for me, and I seriously considered suing. Thankfully, I discovered the manual settings. It took a bit of learning, but now I am able to close my eyes and spin the dials and focus adjustment until there's virtually no chance of a picture that leaves nothing open to misinterpretation. Still, it was a very near thing.

There are exceptions to every rule, of course. Sometimes, believe it or not, a sportsman actually lucks into a monster buck or a limit of ducks—not that these things have ever happened to me. I am told that this is the time when you actually want a crisply focussed professional shot, and this makes sense. After all, your wife wouldn't let you send out your Christmas cards any other way.

The real problem here is that you need to rely on a buddy to take the picture, and then, even with an automatic camera, you have to worry about how much ground the term idiot-proof covers. I remember one particular year when the Wanderer bagged a really nice buck. Things like this happen once every millennium in our camp.

"Here," he said, "take a picture of me and Old Hatrack." He handed me his new camera, then propped up the deer's head and smiled like Noah after finally unloading the skunks. "Take your time, now," he advised, grinning widely. "You'll be seeing this for the next few Christmases."

"How do you use this thing?" I asked.

"It's simple. Point and shoot. The camera does the rest."

Well, let me tell you, it didn't do the rest very well if at all. Unfortunately, the Wanderer never took that deer to a taxidermist. Mostly because he and his wife couldn't agree on things. She objected strenuously to the concept of a full-body deer-mount coffee table—some silly concern about it clashing with the moose wall unit. Despite her stance on this matter, she's really a good person. Of course, disputes like this make good photos paramount. So, not long after losing that argument, my buddy and I waited at the mall while that roll of film was being developed.

"At least I'll have great photos," he said hopefully.

"Sure you will," I agreed uneasily.

We picked them up a little while later, and I guess the Wanderer expected a whole lot. Most people don't tip the photo technician.

"I wonder if I can sell them to the outdoor magazines?" he asked.

I stood breathless in anticipation while he fumbled with the envelope like a nervous Oscar presenter, then flipped through the photos, one by one. The look on his face said it all. And, I might add, further supported my theory regarding the true identity of that chimp.

They say a picture is worth a thousand words. Maybe so, but after shuffling through twenty-four blurred images of my thumb, the Wanderer looked my way, gritted his teeth, and just mumbled two of them. Maybe, one day when he starts talking to me again, he'll cough up the other nine hundred and ninety-eight he owes me.

20

THE PORTAGE

WE LAY IMMOBILE ON THE ROCKY SHORE OF THE OLD abandoned landing, mildly exhausted but recovering at a speed appropriate to fellows in their mid-thirties. Vultures circled patiently overhead, possibly mistaking our beer bellies for bloating.

The paddle that got us there had been a difficult one, spanning the breadth of two long Canadian Shield lakes, with the wind speed and waves reminding me of a wedgie—coming straight up the middle, disturbingly high and fast. With two days left in the trip, I decided it was a thought best left unsaid.

Ahead of us was an overgrown portage route. Like every one I have ever encountered, it was on a formidable uphill grind that was several hundred yards long and wound through an impenetrable boreal jungle. For some reason, possibly having to do with conservation, they don't make open, level, fifty-yard trails to secret lakes with great brook trout fishing.

According to the word of mouth that had inspired our expedition, this heavily foliated stairway to heaven supposedly led to a tiny backwoods lake that was cold, clear, deep, and full of uneducated brookies. Looking back, I find it odd that we trusted a fellow fisherman for directions to an angling Shangri-La. Normally, those who wet a line are furtive, devious types, especially about secret honey holes, and when I paid for his eighth beer and thanked him profusely for finally releasing the information, I reminded him to beware of such folks.

Looking upward, we prepared to tackle this northern Ontario mini-Everest. I looked at my partner and he looked at me, and I suppose we both saw a sucker. Hence, the bet.

When you travel in the bush long enough with the same person, you begin to think that you know him. And when that person is your brother, you are doubly sure. As siblings, you will sooner or later decide to apply that knowledge to some nefarious end. All in the name of good fun and a decent tale to tell somewhere down the road, when it is once again safe to laugh aloud. Which is normally not the case at the time.

It has often been asserted that great minds think alike and fools seldom differ. Therefore, Martin and I had it beat either way. So, naturally, we looked at each other with variations of that same malicious grin that Dad had made his trademark. Since we each knew the other's weakness (mine sloth and his greed), we began the elaborate ritual of fishing the other guy in.

"Doesn't look like too bad of a hike," Martin said, grinning like a hungry cat in a crowded pigeon coop.

"What? Are you crazy?" I shrieked calmly. "It's a mile of tangled tag alders and burdock covering a rocky trail that a mountain goat couldn't negotiate. And all uphill to boot." Then, setting the bait, I added, "It'll take us half the day to complete."

"You are such a wimp," he declared.

"Am not," I whined.

"Betcha I could portage all our gear up to the top of that hill in less than an hour," said my younger, stronger, and obviously more

ambitious brother. When given a chance to flex his testosterone, Martin rarely balked.

"An hour, you say?" I confirmed, suppressing a smile.

"Yes, that's when the big hand goes all the way around," he explained.

I looked at him like he had taken one too many fast balls to the head, then thanked God that Dad always let me be the pitcher.

Hesitating just long enough so he would think he was on the winning edge of the bargain, I extended a handshake, and we settled on a suitable dollar value—should he succeed. Avarice and macho determination shone in his eyes. As for me, I thought it was a bargain at twice the price. My shoulders and back would be eternally grateful, and whatever money I lost would be that much less weight to carry on the way back.

With the formalities completed, we began. I walked up the hill carrying my watch and a sense of all being right in the world. Behind me, Martin was laden like Atlas, carrying our canoe, pack, food bag, paddles, water, fishing rods, and the like. He looked like a pack mule, and I told him so, although I used different wording, feeling that I could probably outrun him just then.

From under the canoe, he let out a wolflike snarl. Which is perhaps what made the doe leap from her bed and crash off, tail flagging, branches snapping, and horizon beckoning.

"A deer!" I yelled. Those things never fail to excite me.

By the time Martin's head was extracted from the yoke, I was saying to forget it. The bounding doe was lost in the summertime foliage.

Just then, something caught our eyes. Two good, velvet-antlered bucks were sneaking off in the other direction. Had we been predators, the doe would have caused a life-saving diversion for these two. Not very chivalrous, I thought. And as I smiled, it was easy to imagine the doe thinking the same.

After that memorable moment, the terrain got rougher and the footing less stable. It wasn't easy watching my brother suffer like that. After all, he was my flesh and blood. So I took a drink from my canteen and sauntered on ahead where I couldn't see him.

Within minutes of the deadline, I watched him stumble to the top of the ridge, sweaty, scraped up, and exhausted. There, I speculated, but for the grace of God go I.

Martin reached the end of the portage despite the burrs, snags, slick rocks, mud, and his very heavy load. I was quite surprised.

Neither the trip wires placed on the trail nor the rocks in my pack had slowed him down at all.

"I did it," he gasped happily from beneath the canoe.

"Yes, you did," I admitted.

Reluctantly, I reached into my pocket and tossed him a two dollar coin.

"Here you go. You won," I said. I wasn't sure if I should show happiness or even provide a ten percent tip. The etiquette in a situation like this is sort of hazy.

"Yes, I won," he answered proudly. He dropped the gear, wiped off some sweat, then bit the coin for veracity.

"Was it worth it?" I asked, unable to control a smirk.

"It was foolish and didn't pay near enough," he said sheepishly. "Still, I'm two dollars richer."

"I guess you feel like that doe then?"

"Huh?" He asked.

"Yeah, it's probably the last time either of you will do that for two bucks."

The water was indeed cold, clear, and deep. And, as I entered it headfirst, I swear I saw squaretails scattering.

21

DUCK CAMP
DEMOCRACY

I T WAS CHORE TIME AT THE OLD DUCK CAMP, AND ZOOM, OUR
camp patriarch, was not overly impressed. Experienced as he
was, he still somehow made the fatal mistake of falling asleep on
the couch, thereby allowing the rest of us to divvy up the mountain
of work that had accumulated after three days worth of hardcore
waterfowling. To those unfamiliar with hunt camps, this is the equivalent of trusting a cop with your donut. It's a rookie's mistake.

Of course, the manner in which his peaceful nap was terminated
didn't help brighten up his ugly demeanor, either. Since there were no
alarm clocks handy, we opted for the next best thing to placing one
right beside his ear. A large slab of peanut butter was smeared uncer-
emoniously under Zoom's prominent beak. Naturally, this impeded
the progress of his last snore, thereby putting an abrupt end to his
repose.

Now most people might find this unusual, perhaps uncomfortable, and maybe even slightly annoying, but to Zoom this was reason
enough to come up swinging, hissing, and spitting like a tomcat hung

by the tail over a water barrel. He hated peanut butter with a vengeance that told me he must have been a peanut in a past life. Crunchy or smoothy, it mattered not. The smell alone drove him mad.

Needless to say, we all knew of this fatal flaw in his character, and from time to time we exploited it strictly because we were lacking a VCR or were bored with cheating at cards. Personally, I always thought this behavior was rather immature, and I even told him so when he finally caught me hiding in the closet, although I am not altogether sure that he understood my muffled arguments as they passed through my constricted windpipe.

I mention that little incident only because I find it highly amusing, and it sort of portrays Zoom's mood better than any other words I could think of. To summarize then, he was not very happy, and he had not changed his opinion of crushed peanuts. For my own part, I saw this bright light. . . .

It took awhile for the guys to separate his bony hand from my newly reconfigured throat, and when the operation was finally complete, I wasn't altogether sure that my Adam's apple wasn't reduced to applesauce.

"Did you see the way Steve turned blue?" asked Ron.

"Yeah," said Danny thoughtfully. "He looked like a Smurf."

This conversation went on ad nauseam even as I reshaped my larynx to a more serviceable form. By this time, Zoom had emerged from the washroom, his face clean and bereft of all traces of the demon peanut. He was hardly recognizable. Still, he looked sort of mean, almost like a Rottweiler in need of a root canal.

Thankfully, Danny drew the short straw. From a safe distance we watched as he approached the old codger cautiously, the way you would a wounded grizzly sow. Smiling ever so politely, he quickly passed the humorless old fellow the scrap of paper that held his assignment. Despite the niceties, Zoom received this with very little grace. Then again, that paper airplane had an awfully sharp point.

"How did I get stuck with that job?" he sneered after dislodging

the paper dart from his forehead. The smell of peanut butter and fear hung heavy in the air.

"Democracy in action," I coughed.

"What d'ya mean by that, idiot?" he responded angrily.

We all answered at once, and the result was unintelligible. However, after a brief huddle we determined that in this particular case, the idiot and I were one and the same. The burden of leadership was therefore mine. (Coincidentally, my wife has often maintained that I am a beast of burden as well, only she phrases it differently.)

"What I mean is this: There were several jobs needing the camp's attention: dishes, firewood, tidying up, and the like. So those of us who attended our little discussion, bid and voted for their disposition." I stated this in the most pompous voice I could muster. In the background, the boys demonstrated approval and a rudimentary understanding of parliamentary procedure by yelling, "Here, here!" Except for Big Ron, who, having regularly skipped political science classes, didn't quite understand the concept. He shouted, "There, there!"

"But what kind of job is this?" Zoom pleaded as he waved the horrific to-do list like it was the last sheet of toilet paper in camp.

"It's not a pretty job, to be sure," said I, "but it is vitally important to the morale of this camp."

"But. . . ." he countered suavely.

"Do you remember saying, 'No job is menial if it is done with pride and craftsmanship?'" I interrupted, reminding him of an earlier discussion.

"But it's not even my @#$*& dog!" he screamed, pointing at Roxy, Dan's overworked and apparently overly regular chocolate Labrador retriever, who lay innocently dreaming of multiple mallards dropped near the blind.

"But it is your lawn," I countered.

By now all the others were at their prescribed stations, happily washing and drying or tidying up as they had been ordered. Everyone was whistling while they worked—kind of like the Seven Dwarves with each vying for the coveted role of Dopey.

There's nothing like the misfortune of others during hunt camp. Even Roxy took to washing herself in that interesting way only pets can. No doubt she snickered between the accumulation of hair balls. Zoom recognized defeat, having experienced it more so than the rest of us. He opened the screen door and reached for the shovel propped just outside. Having always maintained that discretion was the better part of just about anything, I stepped back behind Ron.

I guess we were all a little nervous. The last time something like this happened, Zoom went postal and licked every stamp in the cabin. It was the first time we'd ever been forced to send postcards to our wives. Now they practically expected it.

"Democracy stinks," he mumbled softly, which was ironic in light of the job that he faced.

With that he walked outside and began his distasteful chore. The group of us breathed a collective sigh of relief, then gathered by the window to watch while Ron made the popcorn and poured the drinks.

When Zoom returned a few minutes later, we were scattered in reclined positions on the odd assortment of furniture that is the hallmark of every good hunt camp. No one said a word.

"Did you have to feed the dog so much peanut butter?" he whined, looking for the perpetrator of that inspired act.

I buried my face in a magazine and was surprised to note that everyone else did the same. Silence descended upon the room.

"All right," he said dejectedly. "It's over. Just tell me whose idea this was."

We all looked at each other for a minute or two and smiled.

"Let's just say it started out as a grass roots movement," was the response.

22

A Stitch in Time

LL'S FAIR IN LOVE AND WAR. BUT WHEN IT COMES TO THE hunt, things can just get plain nasty. There's really no telling what an unscrupulous outdoors person will do just to obtain bragging rights. In a way it's pathetic, and it almost makes me wish I was born with talent instead of guile.

I said as much to Noreen, the blue-haired woman at Fabric Land, and she nodded sagely between sensuous sips of hot milk. Noreen knew the score. She'd been around. After all, she had been outfitting us boys ever since we accidentally discovered that her store carried a complete line of camouflage fabrics and accessories. From Polar Fleece to Thinsulate, it was all there. And staffed by pretty sales women to boot, Noreen and her alluring liver spots, notwithstanding.

Entering this feminine den of pins and needles, a grizzled old hunter felt as helpless as a sheltered teen-age girl driving daddy's old clunker in for a tune-up. If you didn't have sales help you could trust, you'd leave with ten yards of Advantage Camo to make a pair of mitts. But I trusted Noreen implicitly. The batch of tea biscuits I

had brought was just to make sure—
the cost of doing business I suppose.

I believe I am responsible for the
wave of testosterone that now regularly assails the store prior to and during
each hunting season. I had unwittingly
stumbled into the store with my wife
shortly after buying her a new sewing
machine. As my head did a two hundred
and seventy degree swivel while inadver-
tently tracking the movements of a curvy young saleswoman, I
practically tripped over a bolt of Cabela's Marsh Grass in cotton.
This is not the sort of thing you do in front of your spouse, by the
way. The ensuing ruckus only ended when she got distracted by a
linen sale over in aisle five. It was then that Noreen came to my aid,
and I'll never forget the way she gingerly removed the Velcro from
my eyebrows. From that day on, we got along just fine. Naturally,
word got out. It's a small town.

By autumn the place was a regular hangout for us well-dressed
outdoorsy types, and a few of the hardcore boys even bought sewing
machines. If a fellow kept his mouth shut and ears open, he could
learn a thing or two as well.

While looking for a new fall pattern for a bow hunting parka, I
whispered, "I heard the Wanderer was in." I smiled conspiratorially
and slipped Noreen a fresh biscuit and a pair of support hose.

"Yes, I believe he was. Shirley says he bought three yards of Real
Tree fabric in Polar Fleece. She's such a gossip," she giggled.

"Hmmmm . . . hunting the hardwoods. Just as I suspected." The
Wanderer had tried to tell me that his deer stands were in the cedars.
I laughed out loud. His deceitfulness was shameful. Besides, I knew
his lie from the outset. My stand, the one he thought was at the end
of the small marsh, was in the cedars. Was there no honor left?

"The biscuits are grand. Good for the digestion, too." Noreen
winked. "Perhaps for another one, I might remember something

equally important." Her waxy skin glowed sallow like a Coleman lantern through the walls of a yellow tent.

"Did he say whether he hunted low or high?" I asked, as I offered her more baked goods. I tried to stay cool, as if it were all so unimportant.

She looked me in the eye, her dentures gleaming white under the fluorescent light of the cutting table. "Let's just say he bought elastics for all of his pant hems."

I smiled. So, his hemline was up this year. Obviously, he was trying desperately to avoid burrs. This told me that the rat was hunting low. Suddenly, it dawned on me. Of course, the hardwoods by the swamp. It all made perfect sense now.

"Did he mention anything else?" I asked, trying not to seem too anxious.

"Well, he asked about you," she whispered as she dusted the dandruff from my shoulders and straightened my collar.

"Did you say anything?"

There was silence. The smell of A535 and hair spray hung heavy in the air.

She gave me a grandmotherly smile. "No, I didn't say anything."

I couldn't believe his audacity. Now he was asking about me. He even stooped so low as to use a sweet and innocent old woman to get the dope on a hunter and the big buck he'd staked out. Friend or not, I'd have to watch him closely from here on in.

I gave her another biscuit for her troubles, then sauntered over to the cash. As the smiling young woman rang in the fabric, pattern, buttons, and matching zippers, I searched for my preferred customer card. She smiled, finally recognizing me without the Velcro monobrow.

Just then the Wanderer walked in, whistling a Lawrence Welk tune, bearing Geritol and a daisy. Seeing him first, I ducked behind the crotchet needle and zipper display.

"Noreen!" he called out merrily. "That zigzag stitch you recommended was just the ticket! And just to show my gratitude, I brought you these. As he hugged her, I noticed he was wearing a new camo smock that was almost identical to mine.

I got up and walked over to confront them. In my head, an old seventies song flashed back: "I will survive. I will survive. . . ."

Suddenly, Noreen looked at me, I at her, the Wanderer at us both.

"Oh, so this is how it is?" I spoke quietly, fighting back the tears.

"It's not what you think," she answered uncomfortably.

"I suppose this explains how you found my secret mallard pothole!" I snapped at the Wanderer.

"Did you think I just stumbled onto it? For God's sake man, it's three miles into the marsh!" He laughed defiantly as he stepped away from her. "And no doubt," he added accusingly, "this is how you discovered my tree stand in the oaks?"

"Noreen," I said sadly, "how could you? I thought we had something special here. I even baked you biscuits!"

"And I brought you Maalox!" said the Wanderer dejectedly.

The old vixen hung her silver head in shame and ambled off into the lace section. She never looked back.

Shaking my head, I surveyed the store one last time before I walked out, ripping up my preferred customer card as I went. The Wanderer, saddened as he was, joined me.

Later, after a friendly duck hunt, my old buddy asked how we could have both been so stupid. The shooting was good, so I gave him the short answer. "It was easy," I said. "After all, Noreen always said we were both cut from the same cloth."

My buddy nodded, knowing that even if this weren't entirely accurate, at least it carried a more than a thread of truth.

23

MUDDY WATERS AND THE RAINBOW BLUES

SOME TIME AGO, WHEN I WAS ESSENTIALLY A SACRIFICIAL VIRGIN, ready and willing to be hurled down that fearsome volcano known as fly fishing for steelhead, I stood happily on a slick creek bank. In front of me was an early spring creek, blown out from the runoff of melted snow. As ice floes capable of sinking the Titanic glided by, I readied my fly rod and dreamed optimistically of big fish holding fast in the raging torrent at my feet. If ignorance is bliss, I was ecstatic. I knew nothing of the sport. Ten years have passed since then, yet my buddies will tell you that some things never change.

My cold, awkward fingers had just finished tying on a No. 10 Mickey Finn streamer, a fly much brighter than me, when a shaggy stranger approached. His noisy little lap dog, which was not noticeably bigger than a fair-sized muskie lure, seemed to be walking him. Somewhere beneath all of that hair was a set of vocal cords that would put a pack of coyotes to shame. The dog was loud, too.

"Creek's kind of muddy," the stranger stated in the kind of advisory greeting that could only come from an expert armchair angler.

Of course, in the spring, when rainbow trout are up and running, everyone who offers advice considers himself a fisherman on par with Captain Ahab. This fellow didn't have a peg leg or white beard, but I recognized the type nonetheless.

I looked at the fast water again, and, sure enough, it was still brown. I then agreed with this Master of the Obvious, politely smiled, and continued readying my gear while trying to look absolutely impressed with his advanced grasp of color theory.

"You won't catch anything today," he stated, apparently for my listening pleasure. "Not with the creek like that."

"Probably not," I agreed, "but I fish when I can." With that I nodded curtly and carried on stepping knee-deep into the flow, hoping that he would forget that he wasn't wearing waders and follow me to continue the conversation.

"I was gonna fish today," offered this riverside motivational coach, strategically positioning himself on the high bank behind me, perfectly in line with my back cast. "But I saw the way the water looked, and I knew there wasn't a chance. You won't catch anything. No visibility."

"Yeah," I responded testily between gritted teeth, "but you don't know if you don't try." Then I turned my attention to the pool.

He stood behind me, dodging back casts until the little dog lost interest and dragged him away, at least giving me a reason to call it man's best friend, whatever it was. Well, I thought, at least one of them got the hint. Normally, I don't mind company, especially when the talk turns to fishing or hunting, but back then fly fishing for steelhead was new to me. I had used fly tackle on panfish, bass, and brook trout for years, but never once for the Lake Ontario migratory rainbow runs in the spring. I needed some quiet time alone.

I took a quick glimpse around, then cast my red and yellow fly into the murky depths of the pool before me. A half-hour later I was learning everything about steelhead fly fishing that the books don't divulge. For example, steelhead flies love trees and are, in fact, attracted to them. And sometimes my ears look like trees to them.

Within the next hour I began to formulate a simple solution to this problem. Avoid trees and other forms of plant life. This meant choosing my spot with the kind of care that your wife reserves for those times when you have a new and very heavy couch slung across your aching back. It wasn't long before I found the spot. Lesson one was learned.

Soon after, I witnessed something I had never seen before or since. Possibly in an effort to avoid me, a big and obviously suicidal steelhead buck ran hopelessly aground like an aluminum boat full of sumo wrestlers. As luck would have it, Dorothy and Toto returned just in time to watch me revive and release this directionally challenged and totally stunned fish.

"Got one, I see," he said with transparent envy and surprise.

I nodded, unable to lie but not particularly inclined to be accurate.

"That's a big fish for such a light rig. How many did you lose?" He suddenly laughed.

"Twelve," I stated flatly. By that I was referring to the number of flies I had snagged in my efforts to defoliate my surroundings. I think he misunderstood me, because fifteen minutes later he was back at the creek with a heavy fly rod in tow. I prayed that he'd tie on the yapping dog and try for a really big one, but I knew it wasn't to be. The little dust mop would be too hard to roll cast. Instead, in an uncanny act of coincidence, the expert tied on a Mickey Finn.

The rest of the day saw me wading upstream with him and the dog always shadowing me one pool back. It was time spent casting flies, losing flies, retying flies and leaders, and expanding my once-innocent vocabulary each time I waded into a deep, previously undiscovered hole. My frayed nerves left me wondering at what point the relaxation part was to begin.

By late morning, though, I was at that starting line. The sun had cleared the heavy clouds and was shining brightly, and I had a nice pool entirely to myself. Even the trees and wind were unusually forgiving, having probably decided among themselves that harassing me was like taking candy from a baby. I began casting like I really knew how, and it was heavenly. The whole situation was as rare and beautiful as a Porsche in a trailer park.

Of course, the water was still brown, and the fish were well hid-

den, if they were there at all. This last point was contentious.
Nevertheless, I was truly happy. With or without the fish I was fly
fishing well, and I was in the groove. If you're like me, you learn to
treasure these moments. So it came almost as a total surprise when the
dorsal fin of a very large fish suddenly broke the water in the shallow
riffle just below where my streamer hung in the current. Then it headed toward my fly like a freight train on rocket fuel. My heart pounded like Rocky in a meat locker.

Now, it's my story, so I could lie to you and tell you how that
behemoth took my fly, peeled off my line, and finally succumbed to
my angling mastery. But it wasn't to be, and besides most people are
not that gullible. Instead, that fish torpedoed past my fly and left me
brokenhearted. Not since my discovery that women generally don't
lust after short, balding men had I felt so downhearted. I tried awhile
longer, but the rest of that day was anti-climatic. There were no bragging rights to be had.

On the way out, I passed another fellow. He nodded and asked
the universal question, "Any luck?"

"No," I said.

"I suspected as much. The creek's too muddy," he retorted.

Not in the best of moods, I pointed to the portly fellow and his
dog at the next pool down, who was now frustrated and flailing the
brown water to a creamy froth. "I really think you should go down
there and tell him that."

24

RUNNING WITH A BEAR BEHIND

BACK AT THE OLD HUNT CAMP, MARTIN WAS FIT TO BE TIED. While the rest of our gang returned from the evening shoot with nice bags of birds, he and Zoom didn't have enough feathers between them to tickle a deer mouse. In fact, they had barely hunted at all, which was odd. They had drawn straws and won our best blind, the one we called Thumbwrecker. Situated on a point at the mouth of a narrow creek, this driftwood and cedar blind never failed to put its gunners in the middle of great shooting opportunities. It also held some fond memories for the boys of our camp. It was the place where Zoom first learned to use a sledge hammer.

Martin and Zoom had left with a boatload of optimism, promising to return with two limits of tasty wood ducks. But something went terribly wrong, and as the words spilled out, we soon pieced it all together. Up to a point.

From what we could gather, shortly after setting out their decoys, they beached the boat and got comfortable in the blind. It was then that they noticed a small black dot in the distance. Shambling down

the shoreline toward them was a bear. That's where their stories part-
ed ways.

In a way, this is understandable. Any outdoorsman will tell you
that bears are sort of like traffic accidents—no two people ever witness them the same way. Still, judging from the vast difference in their
tales, you would have had no choice but to assume that Martin and
Zoom were both asleep at the wheel from the moment that the bruin
sauntered into their lives.

To avoid confusion, we silenced Zoom, then took seats at the old
table. Big Ron and Zoom settled on the couch. While coffee was poured,
our little kangaroo court of public opinion asked Martin to present his
case. We assured Zoom that we would remove the duct tape when it was
his turn, proving once again that while justice may be blind, it's not necessarily deaf. From beneath Big Ron, he uttered muffled approval.

Martin began auspiciously. "Gentlemen, we had just entered the
blind after placing the decoys. Naturally, I was looking forward to a
fine hunt, despite my unfortunate choice of partners. We agreed on
our posts. I watched up the beach and the creek, while Grizzly Adams
over there faced down the beach and covered the lake. A minute later,
I noticed a black blob moving toward us. Once it got within two
hundred yards, I immediately recognized it for what it was: a bear.
Naturally, I told Zoom."

He paused, shook his head, and grimaced. "That was my biggest
mistake. I was closest to the exit, and before my warning was finished,
I found myself flat on my face with size nine imprints across my back.
Down the beach, I saw a cloud of dust, the kind the Roadrunner
makes. The old fellow made record time to the boat. Ben Johnson
never moved so fast, steroids or not.

"When I rose and removed the sand from my teeth, I looked
toward the bear, which was now about eighty yards away. He saw
Zoom and stopped cold, perhaps because he realized he had no
chance in catching anything that moved so fast. I fired a round of
birdshot into the air. The bruin turned tail and ran off, although not
nearly as fast as Zoom.

"Then I went to the boat to retrieve Old Yeller. There he was, his head under the seat, like a moronic ostrich. The last time I saw anyone shake like that was when we hooked up Ron's electric toothbrush to the car battery. No amount of cajoling, cussing, or shaming would get him to finish the hunt."

So ended Martin's tale.

Ron got up and applauded. Zoom was released and untaped, and he made a simple and elegant gesture to indicate that Martin had lost his grip on sanity. Then, with all eyes on him, he spoke. "Look, when I saw that little bear approaching, I hardly gave it a passing thought. But, coincidentally, just as that harmless animal picked up the pace, I realized that we didn't have all the decoys out. One was still in the boat. Now, as you know, that isn't right. So, I jogged to the boat and started looking for it. Sure, with that wind off the lake, it might have looked like I was kicking up sand. And to be fair, Martin's glasses were kind of muddy after he fell. Can't blame him for thinking I had run. He banged his head pretty hard when he hit floor. He's a bit clumsy, as we all know."

Martin growled and Zoom flinched, purely out of instinct.

"Anyway, the next thing I know, Martin takes a shot into the air. I thought it was at a duck, and so I naturally figured more were in the sky. Now, you know me. I'm a duck hunter through and through, so I did the only acceptable thing when birds are in the vicinity: I got low, hid, and prayed for dear life.

"Yeah, I was under the seat, but where else are you gonna hide in that little boat? While I was there, I found that decoy, too. As I stretched for it, I suppose I strained my back. Boys, I haven't been in that much pain since I built that blind," he said, holding up his mis-shapen thumb.

"That's where Martin came into the story. Here I am, beneath the seat, trying to reach for this decoy. By the way, the whimpering was due solely to the back injury. Mart kept making a big deal about the bear being gone, as if that mattered to me. He then suggested that we go back and finish the hunt.

"You know me, boys. Nothing would have suited me better than to go back to that blind and hunt until half an hour after sunset. It's not that walking a couple of hundred yards to a boat, in pitch dark-ness with cased guns, while a big bear prowled in the area would both-er me. Unfortunately, I had to decline. I was in serious pain and was-n't as up to wrestling with a bear as I would be in normal circum-stances." He winced dramatically for effect.

As Zoom took a deep breath, we stood back anticipating the further growth of his nose. From around the cabin, we shook our heads and snickered.

"Now," our erstwhile Davy Crockett continued, "you'll have to excuse me while I attend to a special session of laundering some of my white undergarments. And, by the way, tomorrow, I will hunt in the middle of the lake from the boat blind."

25
PACK MULES

THE ECHO FROM THE SHOTS HAD BARELY CLEARED THE HARD-wood hills when I stumbled upon the outstretched, almost lifeless carcass. Lying there was the joyous culmination of a moose hunt. It was just as I imagined, too, a wild, horse-faced beast with thick patchy hair exuding the raw smell of the swamp. I approached cautiously, rifle at the ready, then poked it in its ample hindquarters with a willow gad. Past experience told me that a hunter could never be too careful.

Reuben Heycede rolled over slowly, wheezing like Barry White after an aerobics class. He wasn't exactly happy with me.

"Quit stickin' me," he whined. "That thing's sharp." Then he smiled feebly and pointed into the thicket. Beyond him, through the tag alders, lay a seemingly dead adult bull moose. Suddenly, and not for the first time, I wished that I'd never known Reuben Heycede.

"There he is," the old bachelor motioned, as if any married person would miss noting the presence of such a large and lifeless beast lying so close.

"Nice shot," I said, after giving it a cursory examination from a distance.

"Yep," he replied humbly from his reclined position. "Where'd I get him, anyway?"

"Between the eyes," I answered.

"But he was running, head down, straight away."

"Exit wound," I clarified.

Heycede always liked to be overgunned.

I walked over to the moose and quickly determined that it was at least as lifeless as the old bachelor, although it smelled far cleaner and was better looking by a long shot. Any deader and it might have been Wawa on a Sunday night in January.

"You really did it this time, Reuben," I said accusingly.

"Couldn't help it," he replied. "He crossed my path as I swung off. I was just trying to scare him out of our huntin' grounds in case one of those new young fellows got any foolish ideas."

"Yeah, well tell that to the old boys," I countered.

Up until that moment it had been a fine moose hunt. There was good company, a bit of cards, some tall tales, and just enough moose sign to know that there wasn't any danger of actually getting one. Who would have figured that a brazen old bull had laid up in the swamp right next door to the camp? Certainly not Reuben, who had decided it'd be a good place for an afternoon nap. Unfortunately, he woke up in the shadow of the gigantic ungulate.

Now, as I dabbed away the tears, I prepared myself for the fun part. It occurred to me that, as far as I know, moose hunting is the only form of "recreation" that places a person waist-deep in a mosquito infested bog so that he might enjoy the simple pleasure of hauling out several hundred pounds of dead weight. And, I thought, after Heycede, there'd be the moose to attend to as well.

I quickly utilized a block and tackle to get the old bachelor to dry land. Being brilliant and resourceful, I then used his birch bark call as a megaphone and began calling in the rest of the party. For a good while there was no response.

"Try the other end," advised Heycede.

"Oh," I responded, finally understanding why my previous efforts at calling moose had failed. Yet, even as my pleas rang through the valley, I still wasn't sure that we'd get an answer. Let's face it, the task of gutting and hauling out a moose is about as pleasurable as, say, the removal of wisdom teeth in a barroom brawl. But, once that moose is down, it's a job that has to be done, usually by everyone but the shooter. So I looked up from the morass and pleaded to all those guys in blaze orange suits who were trying to hide behind the sparse vege-

tation on the hillside. In the end, they
only rushed over because they misunderstood my call of "come here."

"I thought you said you had some
beer," Slim moaned. "I was getting thirsty."

The others concurred, but by the time they
realized the error of their ways, they had mean-
dered far too close to the kill site. The best
they could do was claim an impromptu
ailment. Some began limping, others
held their backs, and one boasted of a
newly discovered allergy to opposing gravity—
as he called it, his million dollar wound. But none held a candle
against Heycede's Academy Award performance, although several
tried to light a fire under him. In matters of lifting, dragging, and
hard work, he was the acknowledged master of avoidance.

"I'd love to help, boys," he moaned heroically, stifling manly tears
and hobbling along, "but I believe I ruptured my spleen as I fended
off that big bull's amorous advances. But even that wouldn't stop me
if I hadn't sprained this ankle while trying to pack him out on my
own."

Now, there's a strange phenomenon that anyone who hunts
moose knows about. Simply put, the pleasure derived from shooting
a moose is inversely proportional to a hunter's proximity to the firing
pin, especially when the only bull tag has just been filled. This is
because the conversion from hunter to pack mule begins as soon as
the chain saw and gutting knives are brought forward. That's why you
always read that the shooting of a big game animal is a solemn occasion.

As the rest of us began growing ears and braying, Reuben insisted that we fill the chain saw with virgin olive oil he had brought,
instead of the regular vegetable oil, as this was his first moose. It was
the only time that any of us had seen Heycede so free with the long
dollar. From his perch on a nearby log, he directed us as the great ani-

mal was drawn and quartered. By this time everyone had a job. And, to be honest, we were almost enjoying it. If there's anything that will bring out the boy in all of us, it's the chance to misuse a chain saw and hatchet.

It wasn't long before Peg Leg and Nine-toes had the makings of a corduroy road cut in a direct circular path to the nearest truck. Soon the boys were grunting and groaning under the oppressive weight of massive haunches. They carried moose meat, too. It took thirteen trips to gather the nine quarters. All the while Heycede smiled and even went so far as to carry out his own rifle, although you could argue that this was mostly for protection.

Funny how, later that evening, he fully recovered from his moose malady. So much so that he began regaling us with the story. Of course, by then, the camp had almost packed it in, but not before Reuben Heycede got carried away. Far away.

26

BUTTERFLIES

LIKE A NEOPRENE-CLAD VON TRAPP, WHILE CLIMBING THE steep hill toward the parking lot, I paused and looked back at the fading sunset settling over the placid river. If it wasn't for a bout of uncontrolled wheezing and a lack of overtight lederhosen, I might have sang. The hills were alive. Primarily with a happy swarm of mosquitoes that had come to regard me as their own private eatery. The fact that some of them were burping instead of buzzing left no doubt that they had drank their fill. Like a good restaurateur, I smiled weakly and waved goodbye.

Another day of fly fishing in the dog days of summer had slipped though my now anemic grasp like an oil-soaked eel down a Teflon-coated water slide. From dawn till dusk I had flailed the water to a froth and defoliated most of the flora on the riverbank, as is my custom. The next fly fisherman had it made.

Memories of the long day began to pass through the editorial processes of my mind's eye for future reference, since I knew that one day I might have to outdo someone else's ludicrous fishing tale.

In my mind, the legion of bad casts born that day never really happened. The good ones sailed out twice the distance and landed exactly where I wanted them to, even if that did happen to be smack dab in the middle of a cedar tree. Fish lost were simply released from a safe distance, and those caught were recollected as being several times larger than life. The submerged log that I battled with for half an hour was largely forgotten. It was like Mark Twain once said, "When I was younger, I remembered everything. Whether it happened or not." Twain was obviously a fisherman.

As I daydreamed along, dawdling and whistling like one of Snow White's dwarfs on his day off, reality struck once again. This time in the form of a sleek, highly polished white convertible. The parked, immovable kind that hurts a person when he trips over it and jams a fly rod up his nose, butt end first.

With all the grace of a poorly clubbed seal, I got up, blew cork fragments out of my left nostril, then looked around for a credible witness to dispatch. Much to my dismay, there was one in the passenger's seat.

Naturally, she was an incredibly beautiful woman. The kind you only see at moments like this. Bikini-clad, tanned, oiled, and absolutely indifferent to my pain and suffering. It seemed like she was meant for me—except for the bikini-clad, tanned, oiled, and beautiful parts. My marriage also provided a minor hindrance. She looked like one of those models who specialize in poses on the hoods of hot rods. On second look, I realized she had enough parts left over to do my old junker as well. Not wanting to be mistaken for rude, I quickly dislodged my eyeballs from her ample cleavage.

"Hello," I said, nonchalantly picking out the larger chunks of gravel and sod from the gaps in my teeth. Then, wincing seductively, I removed the Elk Hair Caddis fly from my chin, suppressed a manly whimper, and made a mental note to go barbless from now on. I am nothing if not suave at times like this.

Obviously impressed but still playing coy, she shook her long blonde tresses, rolled her lovely blue eyes to the paling sky, glowered

at me, then went back to reading her paperback romance novel. The
sort that never have a wild-eyed fly fisherman sharing the cover with
the heroine's passionate expression and generous cleavage.

Perhaps it is because, as I've been told many times over, skin-tight neoprene waders over a pot belly and under a smelly fishing vest aren't nearly as sexy as a strategically torn pirate suit over a gleaming washboard stomach. Something I still find puzzling to this day.

Despite her choice of reading material, she seemed to be the perfect woman, never having said a word and all. But she looked . . . well, kind of annoyed. My years of sensitivity training, plus the fact that she pouted in a Marilyn Monroe kind of way, made this clear. Incredibly though, she wasn't upset with me. As a married man, I had seen that look enough to recognize it. No, there was something else irritating her. It occurred to me that it might have had something to do with that sixth sense that all women have. The one that tells them that the short, balding fellow is taken, dammit all.

In the midst of all this anguish, her gaze, the one that had pretended to ignore me so effectively, shifted to the edge of the small parking lot, beyond me. As many things are. I turned to see what she was so upset about.

There he was on the edge of the tree line, looking for all the world like the muscular he-man on the paperback's cover. A great big man with great big muscles and a washboard stomach, clad only in shorts, sinew and brawn. He pranced around the fields adjoining the lot while delicately scooping up butterflies with a delicate net. To me, it seemed totally one-sided. I would have laughed out loud, but my Momma didn't raise no dummies, even though many of my acquaintances routinely debate this point. This giant of a man could have killed me with just one of his beefy pinkies. In my defense, I might have deterred a determined attack by bleeding profusely on him after his first shot. It's a strategy that got me through my youth.

"Hello!" he yelled happily as his girlfriend flipped a page and slunk lower into her seat.

"Hi," said I, watching him gently remove a butterfly from the net.

"Fly fishing?" he queried while in midprance.

"Yes. Butterfly hunting?"

He confirmed this with a nod and a gleaming white smile.

"Catch any?" he asked while stalking a monarch.

"Just a couple of small ones," I
replied, eager to witness the ensuing struggle.

"Me, too," he said, proudly
pointing to the bugs he held captive in
a Mason jar.

I felt a dangerous laugh coming on, so I got
into my car. I pulled out of the lot thinking the
thing that people usually think about me—namely,
that it takes all kinds. Now, I'm a fairly open-minded fellow. To each
his own, I say. But there was something really strange about that
whole picture. After all, here was a powerful, virile man wasting his
time chasing butterflies on a romantic summer evening. Flowers were
in the fields, birds were singing their wonderful songs, and his volup-
tuous, sexy, and obviously disgruntled mate was sitting there and only
reading about romance.

It didn't seem right at all. To hell with the butterflies. He should
have been fishing.

27
GNOME ON THE RANGE

REUBEN HEYCEDE LOWERED HIS OLD BINOCULARS AND looked across the field with an indecisive mixture of envy and disgust. Two hundred yards on the other side of the fence line, a big buck eased through an open hardwood, calmly feeding as he went. Heycede gritted his few teeth and pointed a gnarly index finger at him. "There he is again. He's the biggest buck in the whole county, and that old bitty won't let me hunt on her danged wood lot!"

"We'll set up tree stands on your side of the fence," I said calmly. "With some rattling and the right wind, that old boy just might jump the page wire."

The old bachelor farmer laughed bitterly. "Think I didn't try that last year? No sir, that buck is far too comfortable there. What he needs is a good scaring out."

Down toward the concession road, Old Jenny, the owner of that big buck haven, sat sipping iced tea on her back porch. She waved politely.

"I don't understand it, Reuben," I said. "Jenny is as nice a person as you could ever meet, and she has nothing against hunting. Why won't she let you on her property?"

"Ain't it obvious?" he stated, slicking back his sparse, shoe-polished hair. He sucked in his pot belly and smiled disarmingly, exposing his six or so remaining teeth. "That old widow woman is sweet on me."

It took me a couple of minutes to compose myself as my sides gradually stopped aching from the laughter. "I'm sure she has more sense than that, Reuben, but maybe if you just made an effort to be a good neighbor. . . ."

"Good neighbor!" he screeched. "Hell, I'm the best there is. When old Always in Continent ran over and left a package on her front porch, I told her 'bout it, didn't I? Most fellers wouldn't have bothered."

"You might have cleaned it up, too. After all, he is your dog." I countered.

"It ain't like I asked him to do it. And besides, she was mighty rude to me after I pointed it out."

"Only because she stepped in it coming out to greet you," I noted.

"The old fool doesn't watch where she puts her feet. Imagine if I took her step dancing?"

I left Heycede with those warped thoughts, but a week later we ran into each other at the garden center. I, like most men, was being dragged around by my wife. But Reuben was doing this of his own free will, humming a song and pushing a cart full of garden gnomes, spinning plastic flowers, and pink flamingos. This was definitely not his style.

"What gives?" I asked.

"I took your advice, young feller," he said.

"Huh?"

"I'm trying to be a better neighbor. Old Jenny has wanted a nice walking path through her wood lot for years. So, I decided to help her out."

"With those?" I asked incredulously.

"Yeah, believe it or not, she's crazy about this kind of stuff. Think they might scare off a big buck?" He winked knowingly.

As the deer season got closer, he phoned me with regular updates on his ingenious plan.

"The path winds right through the wood lot, and we've placed pinwheels, garden gnomes, and flamingos everywhere," he cackled gleefully. "That old buck won't use that area no more. The river is on the other side—and guess whose wood lot is the next one over?"

I had to hand it to him. The old farmer had killed two birds with one stone. Jenny got what she wanted, and it seemed that we had a shot at the big deer, too. It was a perfect setup.

But the next week, when we met at the coffee shop, he looked glummer than ever.

"What's wrong?" I asked.

"I saw that old buck bedding down in Jenny's wood lot, amidst all them gaudy flowers, flamingos, and garden gnomes," he said sullenly.

"Maybe there just aren't enough to scare him off yet," I suggested.

Reuben brightened up. He even paid for my coffee and left a tip. The waitress, Crazy Suzy, nearly keeled over. Fortunately, she didn't. Otherwise, who would have caught me?

From then on, every time I saw Reuben in town, he was carrying another couple of garden gnomes and some plastic spinning flowers. People were starting to think that the crazy old fool had lost it. I was certain of it.

Two days before the archery season opened, we walked his property line at last light and scouted. From where we stood, Jenny's wood lot looked like a low budget version of Disney Land. We giggled. But suddenly, high upon the ridge, we caught a glimpse of a nice twelve-point rack peaking over the long grass.

"It's no use," Heycede lamented. "He uses it more than ever now. I figure it's because no predator in his right mind would ever go there."

When the big day finally arrived, I pulled into Heycede's driveway well before first light, walked past his dog, old Always in Continent, and stepped into the kitchen. I was fully prepared to hunt for smaller bucks, but Heycede apparently wasn't. There on the table was a note: "Hunt my property, I got a new spot."

This wasn't like him at all. As I made my way to the stand at the field's edge, it occurred to me that Reuben might have slipped over to Jenny's side after all. He wanted that big buck awful bad, and I suspected that he thought he earned it.

At about ten o'clock, my suspicions were confirmed by a high-pitched war whoop. I ran up the field to the fence line and witnessed a sight that I'm sure no deer hunter, before or after, has ever laid eyes on.

Reuben Heycede, dressed as a man-sized garden gnome, was holding his bow high up over his head and dancing around the monster buck, which had fallen between a pink flamingo and a miniature windmill. Somehow, it all lacked dignity.

"I got him!" Heycede screamed, seemingly unaware of the big picture. "Oh, if the boys could see me now!" He leaped up and kicked his pointy little shoes together. For once, we found ourselves wishing for the same thing.

Later, as I helped him field dress the animal, he explained that the night before the hunt, Jenny had finally given him permission to hunt her property. She even gave it some thought beforehand and went so far as to sew him the gnome suit. Talk about specialized camouflage.

Not long after they began courting, and it wasn't unusual to see them attend movies, farm auctions, and local dances together. Heycede even went so far as to act gentlemanly now and again. Which was nice, because, monster buck or not, I would have hated to see Jenny simply get led down the garden path.

28
WORM-EATERS

IT WAS THE FIRST TIME I'D EVER SEEN REUBEN HEYCEDE
genuinely sad while not in the act of repaying a debt. He stood
there, humpbacked, neatly fixing the weights on his puddle duck
decoys, methodically wrapping line up and putting them away. This
sort of meticulous approach to decoy storage was behavior beneath
him—or any other veteran waterfowler—and it was surely a symptom
of some great misery that a hunting buddy might take advantage of.
This saddened me. As repulsive as it seemed, I'd have to show some
tact and sensitivity before I ripped his heart out and giggled like a
schoolgirl.

"Hey, moron, why so upset?" I asked, showing that flair for sensitivity and tact for which I'm known. Even so, I hoped that I hadn't
overdone the whole facade.

"It's that long-legged hussy," he said, as he raised one billy boot
up on the fender of his old pickup truck. I knew things were bad right
then and there. He never did that to Old Millie. The simple act of
putting a foot on her marred that fine finish he had worked so hard

to achieve. When the old farmer finally brought his boot down, he didn't even seem to care that he'd knocked off years of encrusted manure and left a spot where you could actually see the truck's real color. This was far worse than I thought.

"Woman trouble?" I asked instinctively, knowing full well that this was the only kind of trouble that could drive a man this far. And from the backseat, too.

"Kind of," he replied. "Arnie's got himself a new pointer, and she's nothing but trouble."

"Oh, yeah . . . well, any new dog is hard to compete with," I acknowledged, somewhat relieved. "Four legs, a tail, and better table manners than you."

As depressed as he was, I decided to gloss over the parts about breath, good looks, grooming, and charm. I'm not totally heartless.

"Does he have to spend all his free time with her?" There was a hint of jealousy in his voice.

"That bad, huh?"

"Arnie's went and caught the upland bird bug," he answered gloomily. "Can't get him out to the duck blind to save my life."

"Sometimes, a little time apart is good for the relationship," I said.

"Hey, it's not like we were married or something!" he snapped.

"Oh, sorry. I was just rehearsing my lines to Carol. Today's the day I'm going to break the news about deer season to her. Got to thinking out loud, I guess."

"My condolences," he said while patting me on the back.

"Yeah, just when I was getting used to peacetime."

"At least you have a hunt to look forward to," he moaned.

"Well, I hear Arnie's dog is dynamite on woodcock," I countered.

"I knew that no good would come of it. He should have got himself a retriever. But, then again, he never could be normal."

This from a man who wore red suspenders and a straw hat to formal functions.

"Reuben," I consoled, "we all have different roads to travel."

"Yeah, well, Arnie chose a rabbit trail straight through the hawthorns."

I guess it must have been tough on the old guy. Arnold and Reuben had been duck hunting partners since high school, which was part of the reason that it them took eight migratory seasons and a case full of shells to complete the curriculum. By the time they had graduated, they were older than most of their teachers, though none the wiser. When mallards were in the creek, marsh, and back ponds, those two were as inseparable as a campaigning politician and his smile.

But now, Annabella, a Brittany with a nose for timberdoodles and grouse had come between them, and Reuben was taking it hard. After all, who was going to retrieve his ducks and set out decoys?

"Why would anyone want to hunt for woodcock when there are mallards, geese, and wood ducks in the sky?" he lamented.

"Woodcock are fun, too, Reuben, and they are smart as—"

"As smart as what? You wear blaze orange while a hyperactive dog wearing a little tinkling bell leads you straight to them. Then the birds just sit there under his hot breath, hoping he'll go away. How smart can they be?"

"Why not go with Arnold and find out?" I suggested. "Humor him."

"Are you kidding? Me, chase those worm-eaters? Never again," Reuben said.

"You've tried it?" I asked, quite surprised. Up until then, I had always mistakenly associated woodcock hunting with style, elegance, and social graces.

"Hell, yeah. I once hunted them with a fellow from Coldwater. He was right into it, too. He had an electronic collar on his dog that started beeping when she was on point. We followed that silly thing around for two days, through mud, thorns, and swamp edges. All for a chance to shoot a bird half the size of a green-winged teal."

"Sounds like fun. Did you get any?"

"That's not the point," he snapped.

"Well, what is?"

"That beeper conditioned me. For a week after that, every time a truck backed up I'd walk toward it."

"But Arnie's dog only has a bell."

"Great, then I'll be chasing ice cream trucks," he growled.

"That's dangerous." I admitted. "Think of all the kids you'd run down."

He gave me a look that would have cauterized a ruptured hemorrhoid, then called me a name that wasn't far off the mark.

"Sorry," I said. "I'm sure it's not that bad."

"Oh, yeah! That's not the half of it. Woodcock hunting changes a man—and not for the better I can assure you. Arnold has already ordered himself an Orvis upland vest, and I swear that his Brittany is teaching him manners. Would you believe he's stopped calling them partridge? Apparently, they're ruffed grouse now, and he won't shoot them on the ground or in trees any more. Imagine that, after all these years. What's next, calling pickerel walleye? No good will come of this, I tell you."

"Don't you think you are overreacting?" I asked.

"Mark my words, he'll have a fly rod by spring," he shivered. "From there on, it's a quick slide to catch-and-release."

We both winced.

"I still think you ought to go out with him," I advised. "He's real proud of that dog,"

"No way! First off, those brown-feathered bats are either in or they are not. And no one really can predict why. Secondly, they're too small. You'd need a limit to have a decent feed. And no one ever gets a limit. And lastly, they're worm-eaters. Ewwww!" He added further emphasis with retching sounds.

"Reuben, I bet if you went out with Arnie just once, he'd join you in a duck hunt this Saturday."

"No way am I going to chase a worm-eating bird that has a name that sounds like it's part of a cigar store Indian's anatomy," he stated flatly.

"So, you gonna hunt ducks alone this Saturday then?" I asked, halfway hoping for an invitation.

"No, it ain't the same without Arnie. He's got waders."

"What then?"

"Arnold can chase those worm-eaters all he wants," he said with more than a little disgust. "As for myself, I'm going perch fishing."

With that, he drove off to the bait shop while I was left to ponder the difference.

29

CALF TAILS

LITTLE BOB PROPPED HIS PUMPKIN-SIZED HEAD IN HIS BEEFY hands and stared vacantly across the battered barroom table. The whole scene had the makings of a country music video gone bad. Below those sad blue eyes and multiple chins were four empty beer bottles and enough pretzel crumbs to stuff a tackling dummy. Bob was known to eat during times of stress, and by the looks of that dust pile, the whole world must have sat pretty heavy on his powerful shoulders.

I noticed all of this the minute I entered that smoky backroad watering hole but couldn't imagine the cause of it. At six foot four, Little Bob weighed as much as most small Buicks and was generally unflappable. Better still, he wore a perpetual goofy smile and was a hell of a good man with a four-weight rod and a dry fly. Despite this, he remained humble and loved to hear a good hunting or fishing story. As barroom companions went, he was damn near perfect.

I sat down and ordered Canada's finest and a pristine bowl of pretzels. I don't drink all that much, but with a waitress that tough you just don't order lemonade.

"Thelma phoned," I said. "She told me you needed to talk right away."

Bob nodded, shook his head, and gazed longingly toward the battered old trophy of a brook trout that hung crookedly on the wall over the bar. That squaretail was a remnant of years gone by and proof that even if fairy tales don't come true, fish tails just might. No one could recollect where or when that giant brookie was caught, but the fact that it hung there, cobwebs and all, held out hope to all of us lesser mortals who chase those watery fantasies.

Beside it was a dusty old buck mount. It wasn't any credit to the art of taxidermy, either, and like barroom bucks everywhere it had to endure sweaty baseball caps hung from it's fair-sized ten-point rack. But that and the fish gave the place just enough ambiance to make it comfortable for us country sports, with the added reward of acting as natural deterrents to wives, wandering mother-in-laws, and even decent folks. Nothing short of a stay at Devil's Island matched the solitude a man could find there.

"This fly fishing is gonna kill me," he began quietly.

At least he'd die happy, I thought. Why complain?

"Causing trouble at home?" I asked, having had firsthand experience on the matter a time or two. Not that I ever understood why. I mean, when confronted with the option of fishing through a decent hatch or returning home to a romantic candlelight dinner on a kidless weekend, the right path is never really clear, anyway.

"No, but trouble at home will start when the word gets out," he continued. "This is a small county. I ain't never gonna live this down."

"Live what down?" I asked, almost afraid to hear the answer. In a place where a man's wife was very often his cousin, too, what could be so bad?

"Promise you ain't gonna laugh?" he asked, jaw set, fists clenched, eyes fierce.

I'm five foot three. The promise was easy enough to make while in the shadow of those glowering eyes and hard, bulging biceps. My Momma didn't raise any fools. At least not on this occasion. Besides, I had introduced Bob and a few other local boys to fly fishing when I first moved to the county. Most had taken it as a passing fad, mildly interesting but not nearly as efficient as a worm hung under a bobber, a shiny spinner, or even a stick of dynamite, the infamous CIL wobbler, dropped into the lake when the Conservation Officer was out of earshot. To these practical men, fishing was for catching dinner. Style didn't matter, and patience was for vultures. Inexplicably, waving a fly rod, fighting off blackflies, studying aquatic insect life, wearing neoprene waders, and catching palm-sized fish that were most often released didn't really make much sense to these fellows. The fishing vests hardly held enough beer, either.

But Little Bob was different. He read all the sporting magazines, and the art and science of fly fishing fascinated him. So I took him under my tiny wing, and to the best of my limited abilities, I showed him how to cast, fish a stream, and tie flies. He did well despite these efforts. So I guess I was more than a little responsible for his current predicament, whatever it was.

He finished another beer and proceeded to enlighten me. "I was fishing the little creek by Reuben Heycede's place."

"Where it borders his pasture?" I asked, making a mental note of it.

"Yes," he said, almost ashamed for holding out on me. "It holds some nice brookies a little ways in."

I did a double take and, muscles or not, glowered back at the ingrate. If it wasn't for the fact that he was capable of maiming me with just one beefy pinkie, I might have blindsided him and ran like the wind. However, Victoria Crosses are not common in my family tree.

"I was gonna tell you about it, honest. . . ." he said sheepishly.

Sure, I thought, pigs fly and the Pope plays hockey, too. "Go on," I said, sour-faced.

"Well, I was doing okay with those Parachute Adams flies you gave me. Caught an eleven-inch speck and everything." He smiled briefly.

Continue, you Neanderthal, I thought. I even managed to force a congratulatory smile as I nodded. Imagine the nerve, him using my flies to catch secret brookies.

He cleared his throat and continued, "Then I lost my last one on a bad back cast and things died down. Couldn't raise a fish to save my life."

"Yeah, well, fly fishing can be like that," I answered coolly without a drop of sympathy. "So?"

"Well, just then Heycede's little calf trots up to the page-wire

fence that's bordering the pool," he said excitedly, his bloodshot eyes looking off into the distance.

"So?" I repeated, wondering what in hell this had to do with secret brook trout creeks, social ruin, and marital woes.

"I ran out of materials at home to tie the parachute posts. This calf had a beautiful white tail that'd make perfect parachutes. I needed some to tie the flies."

"And?" I said, still unsure how all this could contribute to his problems.

Little Bob took a last swig of beer and spelled it out. "Well, I coaxed that cute little calf to the fence line with my apple, and then I grabbed it by the tail, meaning to clip off just a bit. Just enough to make a few flies, nothing more. But it kicked up quite a ruckus, enough to make Heycede come out. The light was dim, and I figure he misunderstood what I was up to 'cause he brought out the pitch-fork pretty quick."

"His eyesight ain't too good." I added, suppressing a life-threatening chuckle.

"No, but he recognized me," moaned the big man.

"And you were in hip boots and had his calf by the tail through the page-wire fence," I summarized as I tried to draw a mental picture.

"He's hunting for me now," he moaned. "Heycede always thought fly fishermen were weird, anyway."

"What can I do?" I snickered.

Little Bob handed me a handful of the calf tail—pretty stuff, too. "Take this back and explain that I ain't no barnyard pervert. Just an ordinary fly fisherman."

It took a while, but after I ran into Heycede and his posse of riled-up, gap-toothed farmers, I managed to clear up the matter, explaining it all over a beer and a fly tying vise. But Little Bob still takes an awful teasing.

That was last week, and now he's a confirmed wet-fly man who, for some strange reason, doesn't even go near chicken coops. And though I'm not so sure which team the Pope plays on, I do know all the best pools in Heycede's crick. So, although I imagine Little Bob would argue, as sordid as it seemed, at least this tail had a happy ending.

30

THE SLOW COOKER

I T WAS ONE OF THOSE WEIRD AND WONDERFUL DAYS YOU WISH
for and sometimes even get at an old duck camp. It embraced us
with feeling I can only describe as serene and wonderful, sort of
like the one that embraces you after folding a bird that your buddy
just missed with three well-aimed shots.

As the small aluminum boats emerged through the curtain of
river mist, the happy hunters in them wore that special smile reserved
for the traditional greasy breakfast of bacon, eggs, and a second helping of home fries. But an extra tooth or two also showed to pay hom-
age to the wood ducks, mallards, green-wings, and geese that were
ceremoniously laid wing tip to wing tip on the slippery dock. Tired
dogs made their way up to the cabin, and humble stories were told of
the marvels of the migration we had all witnessed that morning in
those lonely backwater bays and creek mouths.

Anyone who didn't know our group would have thought that we
knew what we were doing. After all, sheer coincidence on this scale
is a hard thing to rationalize. I mean, what are the odds of almost

everyone in camp nearly getting a limit and remaining humble about it?

But soon, the humility burned off like the river fog beneath the rising sun, and stories began to fly like BS from a catapulted long-horn. And when the last patty finally went splat, there was that uncomfortable knowledge that there was work to be done.

After breakfast, Zoom, our camp founder, took the reins. Which I thought was funny since horses scared the hell out of him. "Look guys, you go pluck the birds, and I'll do the dishes and get things going with the stove and wax," he said benevolently.

We eyed each other suspiciously, as we do in duck camp whenever anyone volunteers for any job no matter how easy or pleasant. You see, in hunt camps, there is a clear and natural order of things. It's expected that a fellow will try to slack off any time he can, and cleaning birds is no different. Not that those of us with any experience actually clean them. We just sit around, back to back, and brag about our better shots as we pretend to pluck. Those poor souls (and there is one or two in every camp) who are burdened by a work ethic end up doing the job. Sometimes, if a fellow isn't paying attention, he might pluck and clean the entire morning's kill while the rest of the guys snicker.

It was Zoom who taught us this universal truth. And maybe that's why there was a general feeling of uneasiness when he actually stepped up to the plate and offered to do something meaningful. But despite the pall that now hung over the camp, someone had to stay behind and melt paraffin.

In our camp, boiling wax is part of the bird-cleaning process. Rough-plucked ducks are dipped into nearly boiling paraffin, then thrown into cold water. After the wax cools and hardens, it is peeled off, taking the remaining feathers and leaving a completely naked bird, ready to field dress.

It's a simple job, something we had always felt Zoom would be compatible with, notwithstanding the challenges presented by the childproof lighter. Yet no one was ever really comfortable leaving him alone with fire. But we were all in a good mood, so we took the chance.

Thirty minutes later we had finished rough-plucking our feathered harvest on a deserted midriver island. As the outboard whined and settled at top speed, Dan, Mart, Ron, and I looked like genetically modified chickens gone horribly wrong. Fluff and down flew from our clothes and into our wake. At our feet lay a score of ducks and several geese, each wearing fewer feathers than Ron, who was at the stern manning the outboard and collecting the fluff that flew toward him. In spite of this, the plucked birds still looked better, somehow.

"Do you suppose he's even started the Coleman stove?" asked Dan.

Martin put his binoculars up and focussed on the approaching dock, where Zoom stood. "I can't see any eyebrows," he yelled. "He must have."

As we docked, Zoom stood there grinning like an idiot. Of course, you had to look close to tell the difference.

Now, generally, we use enough paraffin to wax the legs of a hardcore feminist. No more, no less. This and a duck fit perfectly inside an old army ammo box that we had drilled and vented. It was Danny who first noticed this wax box sitting untouched on the picnic table.

"Why haven't you started boiling the wax yet, idiot?" he said with all due respect to Zoom, who stood smiling, pipe in mouth, hovering over the cook stove and warming his hands.

"I have, moron," he replied, pointing to a closed ammo box cooking over the blue flames.

Danny's jaw dropped as Zoom snickered at his own snappy comeback.

Then, noticing the wax box that Dan held up meekly, Zoom sputtered the words none of us will soon forget, "Hey Dan, if that's the wax, then what's this I'm cooking on the &%^$# stove?"

It was sort of a primitive IQ test, if you ask me. Those with the higher scores dove for cover sooner. I ended up in the fetal position behind a tree before Zoom's pipe ever hit the ground. It was the same tree that Ron knocked over on his way to the barbecue pit.

Danny and Martin left dry land entirely. Dan opted to watch the impending festival of lights from the bottom of an aluminum boat, while Mart cleared both clothes lines screaming something to the effect of, "We're all gonna die!"

By this time, I'm reasonably certain that Zoom had no dry land in his immediate area, and seeing that all the good cover was occupied, he quickly removed the full ammo box from the burner and flung it away. If not for his unrestrained sobbing and panicked running in circles, it would have looked downright heroic.

From various hastily dug, shallow foxholes, we waited for one hundred twelve-gauge shells to cook off in the sealed metal container. Fortunately, it never happened, as we might quite possibly have over-limited on the flock of geese that passed immediately overhead, as well as several other waterfowl in the general vicinity.

The next day, Zoom's facial tic had subsided to mere violent flinches thanks to our help. Most hunting buddies wouldn't have stopped popping paper bags behind him so soon.

The following afternoon we went out to pluck more ducks. This time the wax box was clearly marked, and despite his protests, Zoom came with us. In fact, now whenever he asks for the job of manning the camp stove, we just tell him to go pluck himself.

31

THE MARSH MECHANIC

Z OOM WORE A SMILE THAT WAS REMINISCENT OF A RIPPLE IN A piss pot. That, combined with the fact that he was modeling a new set of mechanic's coveralls, was more than enough reason for concern. All of our bleary eyes turned toward him.

"Leave that new motor with me and I'll have it spinning like a top," he said to no one in particular. In our duck camp, that was what you'd call an attention-getter.

Suddenly, an uncomfortable silence descended upon the cabin. Cards were dropped, cigarettes butted out, and all midafternoon snoring ceased. I swear you could have heard a shear pin drop. But this was no surprise. We all knew what was coming next. Zoom was about to decommission an outboard.

It was a widely held view that the old hunter, who had slept through a small engine repair course in 1978, was the Dr. Kevorkian of outboard maintenance. Of course, this was only a recent theory. For years, not knowing any better, we grew up trusting in his tinkering. So much so that until we began comparing notes with other duck hunters, we believed that the natural life-span of an outboard motor was two duck seasons or less. Approximately two-dozen dock anchors later, a definite pattern emerged, and being sharp as lug bolts, we finally picked up on it.

It was the same story every year. We'd arrive at duck camp and launch the boats. Zoom would stand on the dock assessing them as they went for a quick run, then, on their return, he'd shake his head from left to right like a dashboard mutt. Meanwhile, he'd don coveralls and grin.

"Boy, they're running rough this year, huh?" he'd say, while brandishing a shiny new socket wrench and the one manual that he relied on for every make, model, and year of outboard. He called that tattered and dog-eared book the Bible. Which, in a way, was appropriate. Every time he brought the book out, we all prayed. The thing was that the outboard in question usually needed a tune-up or maintenance like a golf course goose needs a laxative. Yet, within the hour Zoom would be knee-deep in the water off the dock, searching for a critical part. After that, the motor had about as much of a chance of running as Don Rickles would have at making it to the final episode of *Survivor*. The worst part was that no one could stop him.

It would start off so innocently, usually with him pulling off the cowling and mumbling something about minor adjustments in the upper unit. But before you knew it, parts would be laid out all over the picnic table and dock. In the end, the original problem was generally fixed by attaching the fuel line to the outboard. With this in mind, Dan and Dave looked anxiously at each other, then slipped out the back door, presumably to begin the process of burying his tools again.

"Have mercy," Martin pleaded, hoping to distract him. "It's a brand new motor. It's too young to die!"

"Don't be silly," Zoom replied condescendingly. "Didn't you hear it? Why, it practically purred like a kitten—not a single thump, rattle, or wheeze. It doesn't sound like a normal outboard at all. How are other hunters going to know you're even in the marsh?"

"But, that's how a new outboard is supposed to sound," insisted Ron as he rallied to Martin's defense.

Zoom burst into a knowing laughter. "Yeah, right, smart guy. And I suppose they are not supposed to billow black smoke, either?"

With that he left the cabin, hell-bent for the dock and his next victim. David and Danny returned shortly thereafter, snickering happily. "It's all right, he'll never find his tools," said Dave contentedly, as he scrubbed the dirt from beneath his fingernails. But you might as well have tried to stop the tides.

Less than a minute later, Zoom burst through the door. Wild-eyed and giddy, he was covered in more grease than Sunday breakfast at a truck stop. It didn't take a genius to see that this didn't bode well.

"Thank God for this Swiss army knife that Marie got me for Christmas!" he said to Mart as he rifled through the cutlery drawer. "Now all I need is a bottle opener, an egg beater, and a twist tie, and your carburetor is as good as adjusted! And, you know, I've even got these spare parts left over for next time."

Without a word, an impromptu rugby game broke out inside the cabin, and Zoom was on the losing team. Of course, it didn't help that he was the one and only member of his team. It wasn't exactly a pretty sight.

The next day, while he and I hunted from the big boat blind, he finally broke his silence. Since, I was downwind, though, I would have preferred if he talked to me instead.

"Did something die over there?" I asked, while frantically waving my hand. Men know this to be the sort of insignificant statement that serves to reestablish the lines of open and honest communication. Who says we're not sensitive?

Zoom took the bait. "No matter how much they beg, I'm never going to help those guys with their motors again," he began indignantly.

"I think that was the point behind all the threats and duct tape," I suggested.

"Yeah, well, my eyebrows will grow back. But, mark my words, their outboards will never sputter and cough properly without one of my tune-ups."

I nodded respectfully. After all, I drew the short straw. He was my hunting partner for the rest of the day. Besides, it had been a good hunt, at least for me. Zoom, on the other hand, hadn't fired his shotgun once at the waves of mallards that passed over.

"At least you had the good sense to see things differently," he continued.

"Sure," I said. Who would have guessed he had a spare tool kit in his ammo box? And when he disappeared under the cedar canopy, I just thought he was having his usual midhunt snooze.

"It's not like they said, you know. In fact, I'll guarantee that I'm much more mechanically inclined than a trained seal. Anybody can see that."

He then tried to light his pipe with his new child-proof lighter. After watching a brief but desperate display of ineptness, I intervened and turned his pipe right side up.

"Thanks," he said softly. "You know, you sure are one lucky fellow. I got to your outboard just in the nick of time."

"Sure," I answered. "Now get in the boat and forget about that spring."

Then I pulled on the oars and began the long trip upstream, secure in the knowledge that at least there were some spare parts left over from Martin's outboard.

32

THE ICE SLED

Thrashing through the snow,
in a gale-force powered sleigh,
over ice fields we go,
shrieking all the way. . . .

I
T HAPPENED ON A MIDWINTER NIGHT THAT FEATURED WINDS
cold enough to encourage the development of nasal icicles, a
phenomenon as uniquely Canadian as the corner donut shop
and back bacon combined. To make matters worse, the ice was green-
ish-blue and exceedingly slick, a fact that made me suspect not everyone was carrying Kleenex.

I could attest to these simple truths because the Wanderer and I
shuffled across this bleak terrain, each shivering violently, sneezing
and wearing tusks long enough to cause a walrus envy. But it was not
all paradise. When the Wanderer slipped for the third time, his head
bounced off the frozen surface of the lake, and I'll admit I was worried—mortified even. You never want to scare off the fish like that.

But it's hard to say whether he did. It was all so confusing: first the loud resonant thud, reminiscent of someone dropping a gourd on the kitchen floor, followed by that plaintive yelp that he does so well. Yes, it carried across the lake and shattered the peace of the night, and true, far away, sympathetic coyotes howled a response. But did the walleye hear it? To this day, I can only speculate.

"Will you please try to be quiet?" I hissed while he twitched uncontrollably, making angels in the surface coat of powdery snow.

"Whooo hooo! Haven't made angels since I was a kid," he replied, trying not to act the fool. "Didn't mean to make the noise. Just thought I'd take a rest and get a good view of the night sky."

I would have believed him if he hadn't been face down.

After I helped him up and dusted the snow out of his airways, I pointed once again in the right direction. Good buddies will do that for each other, especially when the bite is on and the other guy is dragging the sled with all the equipment.

"Let's go!" he yelled. "Time is wasting." Once again he began hauling our sled toward the heart of darkness. It was the first ice outing of the year, and we were excited to be on our way to a mythical place where the bait shop owner assured us that the fish would bite and the snow never yellowed.

The sled the Wanderer dragged was making its inaugural run. It was the his pride and joy. He fussed over the project from the end of duck season until late January, which was ample proof that the genetic pool in which he had been spawned was in serious need of chlorination and a good backwash. This was a point I made with uncontrolled laughter as he unveiled this mutated version of Rosebud in his driveway earlier that day.

Essentially, it was an out-of-square plywood box with a huge fishing hole cut out in the floor and a small bench at either end. Clever compartments beneath these benches held all of the gear needed to survive a long foray on the ice. However, since the consumption of alcohol is now frowned upon while fishing, the beer cases remained empty. Instead, an auger, tip-ups, slush ladle, tackle, and minnow bucket were piled on sloppily in a manner befitting a master sports-man. All this was fastened atop a set of mismatched, cut-down cross-country skis and laid under a battered old tarp.

As my mad friend explained, the theory held that once we were over fish, pole attachments and the tarp would be erected to form a windproof barrier. From there on, it was a matter of drilling holes and hauling in walleye hand over fist. Hell, he even had a place for the stringer. Optimism like that is infectious. Then again, so was the Black Plague. I should have known. . . .

With this in mind, we plodded on. Me with compass and flashlight, navigating by the influences of the stars, magnetic north, various subtle landmarks, and intuition—but mostly by the well-used snowmobile trail and lit-up huts ahead, I suppose.

The Wanderer, hauling his heavy burden, was breaking into a sweat. But even though he volunteered to drag the sled and wouldn't accept help, all the groaning and whining was getting hard to take. So I shut up like he asked. I am not, after all, unreasonable.

In a short while, we arrived at a quaint little fishing village in the midst of the frozen lake. Huts of every incarnation were arranged in the sort of haphazard manner that told a man that this was one of the last holdouts against the Martha Stewarts of this world. I belched my thanks to the heavens above, and a loud chorus of assorted bodily functions arose from those brave souls tending lines in the immediate vicinity. As an out-of-doors experience, it ranked right up there with the northern lights.

As we chose a likely spot, the wind started picking up. Quite a bit, in fact. I'm not sure if the term "gale force" was ever mentioned, but smarter souls began packing up and hightailing it for the main-land. One wild-eyed character remarked that only a fool would fish in this weather. Minutes later we had the place to ourselves.

In one of those eerie calms before the storm, the Wanderer and I smiled frozen, gap-toothed grins as he erected the pole attachments, and we soon had the tarp set up—sort of like a sail. What happened next, even Stevie Wonder would have seen coming.

Just then a pressure crack developed that would have shamed a fat plumber. Maria, or whatever name the wind goes by these days, decided that she wouldn't be outdone. A sudden gust swept the ice, filling the tarp with its force. It was at this point that my friend came to the conclusion that perhaps he had waxed the skis too well. Personally, I was impressed by the display of sleek acceleration and raw power, yet the sled kept just ahead of him. But soon the Wanderer landed on the back skis and held on for dear life, as is his custom.

Normally, I would be cheering for the dumb inanimate object at a time like this, but since the sled held all of my tackle, I decided to cheer for it instead. It, after all, was making far less noise than my shrieking buddy.

Together they hurtled forward as one petrified unit. The gaping jaws of the pressure crack were grinning at their imminent arrival, and the Wanderer, sensing this, did the only concrete thing that he could do outside of his underwear. He tipped his fast-moving creation. Not since the Jamaican bobsled team had I witnessed such mastery of ice and machine. He arose looking for all the world like Frosty the Snowman on a bad hair day.

Horrified at this near disaster, I ran over and hugged my tackle box. You never know how much you love something until it's almost gone.

Soon we were fishing on the lee side of the overturned sled, but we quickly discovered that we weren't in a mythical place at all. We never did catch walleyes hand over fist. And as I backtracked on the Wanderer's trail picking up the pieces, I couldn't help but notice a thin line in the snow that was a distinctive shade of yellow.

33

PINE NEEDLE TEA

THE MORNING IN QUESTION WAS AS COLD AS THE PORCELAIN seat in an Inuit's outhouse, but these things will never stop true outdoorsmen from enjoying a refreshing day afield. That's why it was so odd that the Wanderer and I had decided to strap on snowshoes, then hoist oversized backpacks for a simple morning jaunt through our favorite stretch of winter wonderland.

Our reasons were many: to scoff at the first good blizzard of the year, to check for new animal signs, and to put some powdery miles on those nearly virginal and misshapen tennis rackets that were purported to keep our weighty bodies farther up in the snow than they ever had a right to be. Aside from ice fishing, it's as close as any northern boy is ever going to get to walking on water.

For me the motive was partly to prevent my wife from selling this valued piece of winter footwear as "practically new" in her dreaded springtime garage sale. The Wanderer, being a simple soul with a mind to match, just wanted to get some fresh air and exercise. He also wanted to use the practically new snowshoes that he got for a bargain at last spring's garage sale.

"Come on," he pleaded, "it'll be good for you. Besides, I want to see what next spring's model looks like."

Now, I'm pretty much a couch potato in the deep of winter. In January, my outdoor energy is expended for the most part by sitting in an ice hut and jigging as slowly as possible. So the thought of an activity that was good for me almost put a damper on my enthusiasm.

The Wanderer saw my resolve weaken and then preyed upon my worst weakness. "I've heard there are a lot of snowshoe hares in that cedar wood lot along the way," he said quietly, as I waffled.

"Bunnies, huh?" I countered.

Those words, along with thoughts of rabbit stew served fresh from the thermos while slowly jigging minnows in a heated ice hut, were just too much. Call it a weakness, but I like high living.

As always in situations like this, shotguns were carried in a purely defensive capacity. Both of us were vaguely aware of the fierce aggressiveness attributed to the wily rabbit. This line of reasoning was fully inspired by our overactive imaginations, Monty Python, and repeated exposure to the cartoons of early childhood.

We bravely left the cabin using the familiar yet unheralded step-stumble-drop method of snow locomotion. Before long we found ourselves face down in a stand of wind-breaking pines. Coincidentally, it was my wind-breaking buddy who pointed this out. After circling to put him on my lee side, I suggested that it might be time to boil the pail and have a brew of nourishing tea. It's my sincere belief that nothing beats Red Rose for a red nose.

Despite the horrific inner workings of the Wanderer's lower gastrointestinal tract, he was on a health kick. This, as any veteran outdoorsman will tell you, can be a mighty dangerous matter. It causes a man to do things that can only lead to trouble. For instance, dabbling in vitamins, healthy food, and exercise can shock a system that's taken years to adapt to bad coffee, greasy eggs, and fatty bacon cooked over a Coleman stove. It's my theory that the road to hell is not only is paved with good intentions but also with middle-aged joggers with trick knees and displaced hips.

Despite these misgivings, which I verbalized with colorful, nautical phrases that were learned during a misspent youth, the Wanderer offered me a rice cake as I simulated a classic one-match fire by using twelve of them along with a generous serving of lighter fluid. Eventually, that dry rice cake went up like a torch, too. All the while he verbalized an intelligent argument about the benefits of vitamins for the outdoorsman. Not wanting to be outdone, I countered by inhaling a Twinkie, then burping the entire alphabet.

"I don't need all that health food crap you carry," I wheezed, coughing up what I hoped was merely a prize-winning phlegm ball. My buddy's dry-heaving only served to bolster my argument. "No, every time I'm out here in God's country I partake in a delicious cup of pine needle tea."

"Pine needle tea?" he repeated, lunging for the bait.

"Yes, pine needle tea. Without it, I'd still be riddled with scurvy!"

"Scurvy?"

"Yes, scurvy. You know, you look a bit off color these days. By any chance are your gums bleeding?"

"No, uh, um . . . why?"

"Nothing really. But . . . uh, if you die, can I have your hatchet?" I inquired, suddenly looking away and stifling a crocodile tear.

"What's is this pine needle tea and what does it do?" he asked nervously.

"It's a wondrous, flavorful, old-time concoction," I explained. "Why it practically saved the members of the Donner Pass expedition. It would have, too, if they hadn't got hungry."

"Good for you, huh?" he said.

"Chocked with Vitamin C!" I assured him.

With that I had him collect a load of pine needles. He then took to the task of dicing them up as I boiled a cup of water on the little rice-cake fire we had going.

As the water came to a boil, he emptied enough evergreenery into

his cup to make a Yuletide wreath. Being helpful as I am, I directed him to let it steep fully.

After ten good minutes on a rolling boil, I pronounced the drink ready. In truth, in nearby towns downwind, paint was inexplicably peeling off walls of its own accord. The woods were filled with a turpentine-like aroma to be sure.

"So this is really going to taste great, huh?" He grinned like an unsuspecting kid standing before a bowl of cod liver oil.

"It's a wonder they don't sell it in those health food stores you frequent," I replied, knowing full well that at least the hardware stores carried a milder version.

"Well, here's to my health!" he toasted as he downed the warm libation.

Now, I had never seen a man's face turn green before, so this was a new and entertaining experience. Although I thought it a bit much when his head swiveled like a great horned owl, I had to admire him for the way he kept it all down while his face puckered up like a bag of dried prunes.

"That wasn't so bad," he lied as the verdant tinges receded from his pallor. "Now, you try it."

"No thanks," I said. "For my Vitamin C, I'd sooner eat these nice Christmas tangerines the girls packed for us."

And that is just what I did. Of course, it was quite a trick peeling them with mittens on, especially while running full tilt with an overloaded backpack and oversized snowshoes.

34
GLOBAL WARMING
AND THE BUSH

A FEW NIGHTS AGO, I WAS LYING IN SILENCE ON THE COUCH. Unlike the traditional reasons for me being there, this time it was of my own volition. My eyes were closed, and I was contemplating outdoors life in general and physics in particular. To be exact, I was practicing inertia—something I was getting the hang of at an impressive rate. But just as I was about to set some sort of provincial record for immobility, that familiar voice cut through the air like screeching tires in an empty underpass.

"Tired, are we?" she asked between high-pitched cackles.

With closed eyes, I could almost imagine the winged monkeys descending onto her scrawny shoulders. Meanwhile, out in the kitchen, our budgie flapped a few times, and my weary eyes jolted wide open, desperately seeking the nearest glass of water.

"No, I'm not tired at all," I said, outwardly calm. "In fact, I was just formulating a theory about global warming as it relates to the outdoorsman."

"More like you were formulating a snore!" she blurted, totally

insensitive to my wholesome interest in science. I had no doubt that her ancestors thought the world was flat, too. Which I suppose is easy enough to believe when your forefathers hail from Saskatchewan.

I sat up looking forlorn and hurt. Actually, I was forlorn and hurt. In sitting up, I had realigned my weary bones far too abruptly. My back made sounds like an out-of-tune xylophone.

"Perhaps, I'm coming down with something," I moaned.

"Old age, lack of physical exercise, with complications caused by an oversized pot belly and an ego to match would be my best guess," she diagnosed with chilling clinical detachment.

"Nonsense," I wheezed, as I gazed down and began the process of looking for my feet. They were sore and I thought slippers might help. You see, I had just spent the previous day clearing a deer trail through Little Bob's wood lot. It was a much-needed habitat improvement project to be sure, but at what cost? Next time, I thought, let those lazy woodland creatures hire a beaver.

It all started when Little Bob, Slim, and I decided that trails were needed to join the alfalfa fields edging three sides of this large and impenetrable bush. It was one of those things that seemed like a good idea at the time—like a small summertime bon fire in the dry hay field.

We reasoned that the local deer herd used that unhuntable wood lot as a refuge during the shotgun and archery season, and we hoped that by cutting trails through it the little hoofed darlings would benefit from our consideration. There may have also been a passing thought or two about the better hunting opportunities, shooting lanes, and easier routes to drag out the venison that would be ours for the taking next fall. Besides, what else could a group of diehard deer hunters do in January?

Anyhow, during the course of this little expedition, I had made several scientific observations that I am sure would be of interest to most outdoors types, since we are, as a rule, intellectuals. They definitely held my wife's attention as she applied the muscle relaxant.

The first thing we noticed was how hard this kind of work had become as compared to ten years ago, prior to the discovery of global warming. This and the thinning of the ozone layer obviously had detrimental effects on the difficulty factor of clearing bush. Perhaps this best explained the huffing and puffing as well. At first Slim suggested that the aging process might also be part of this equation, but this was quickly discarded before we took a break for our two o'clock nap. The warm milk Little Bob had in his thermos helped us see things in better perspective. And, as we all found out, it was good for our digestion, too.

Global warming also seemed to be wholly responsible for the fact that we sunk a little deeper in the snow this time out. It was evident that this warming trend had a softening effect on the snow. It seemed to have especially accelerated this effect since Christmas. We discussed this phenomenon over Mars Bars, hot chocolate, and leftover turkey sandwiches. Although by the end of this conference each of us had too much food in our mouths to verbalize these thoughts, we all nodded our heads vigorously in total agreement on this point.

While on the subject of science, we congratulated ourselves on the merits of doing this work during the coldest month of the year. True, we had only cut two hundred yards of trail, but as anyone knows, if we tried to accomplish the same amount in July we would have had to cut probably closer to two hundred and one yards, based on the foregone conclusion that heat expands.

Following that, we reminisced about how, in the old days before global warming, we could have cleared trails such as these in one-third the time using only a Swiss Army knife. The kind with the saw attachment, of course. And when one of the younger tagalongs produced one, we were all overjoyed. It was unfortunate that the blade was so dull though; otherwise, we'd have showed him.

At this point my wife suggested (how shall I say this delicately?) that there were pasture patties flying to and fro. She even went so far as to say that we were simply getting too old for this kind of hard manual labor. Which, of course, was utter nonsense, and just to prove it I did a push-up. Just one, mind you. I didn't want to belabor the point.

Of course, as I rose, she mistook my smile and chuckle for a grimace and groan. It's a curse that I share with Clint Eastwood. That and raw toughness. Anyhow, she still wasn't convinced. She'll believe in the anti-aging properties of her miracle creams, and she has absolute faith in the plausibility of a romance novel, but she can't seem to find the credibility in my tales. You'd think I was a politician or something.

I explained all of this to my spouse for her own good, in hope that she would be enriched by my wisdom and experience. Yet, when I told her as much, she spit out her drink, burst out laughing, and sauntered off into the next room. I consoled myself with the fact that true genius often goes unappreciated in its time. And content in that knowledge, I quietly eased back down and had a much-needed snooze.

35

SHERMAN'S GREAT ADVENTURE

I'M GENERALLY NOT AN EASY TOUCH WHEN IT COMES TO HELPING my fellow man, but it's different when a buddy twists your arm by calling in a marker. Such was the case when Harold Peight reminded me of his ordeal at the Ganaraska River last year—a tribulation in which he suggested I was a major player.

Harold said I owed him. "Big time," he snarled between tightly gritted teeth. I really didn't see his point though. Hell, it was opening day, and the way it was packed with guys from the club, anybody could have made that back cast. It was just a fluke that mine caught his hat, and who the heck even suspected that Harold had such a fine toupee? Apparently, a very expensive one at that.

Oh sure, I was the first to point it out. But that's only because I thought I had snagged a flying squirrel. Up until then, it had blended in perfectly with his remaining hair. So the guys had a little fun with it. Big deal. Harold shouldn't have taken it so hard. Everyone ought to have a nickname. Even dignified types like the "Widgeon." I thought that was kind of funny, even if he didn't. Get it? Baldpate? Widgeon! Ha!

Anyway, the Ganny fishes pretty well. It would take a lot more than a thrown rug to get me to swear off of it for life. And the boys in the club tried to make it right. They developed a new streamer called Harold's Fury. The chief ingredient is the very hair from that hand-woven toupee. You'd think a guy would forgive and forget after efforts like those. But no! The Widgeon was out for blood. One day, out of the blue, he phones me and says he wants me to do him a favor. Apparently, his wife's nephew, Sherman, was visiting for the summer. He asked if I could take him for an outdoor adventure, adding that Sherm needed the knowledge.

Now the Widgeon didn't exactly adore his wife's family. I knew that much. But Mildred ruled the roost. At ninety-six pounds, and with arms like apron strings, she inspired subservient terror. Sherman would go camping if only because Mildred had ordered it. And I was to be the guide—or else—threatened bald Harold. After all, I owed him.

Later, I was to learn that Dr. Sherman Q. Milqueboné was not exactly the outdoorsy type, but Harold alleged that we would get along fine. After all, the Widgeon maintained, Sherm was a Harvard man with a doctorate in fine literature, and what I did could loosely be described as the written word. What he didn't tell me was that Sherman was cultured and mannerly, loved opera, and could—and would—quote long Shakespearean soliloquies for the sheer hell of it. Like I said, the Widgeon was out for blood.

Mildred had convinced Sherman to broaden his horizons. And Harry naturally thought of me as he felt that the sun never set on my stupidity. Before I knew it, I was the leader of a "simple little paddling excursion," much like in that movie *Deliverance*. Apparently, Sherman wanted to experience a trip like this so he could better understand the work of Thoreau. Me, I just wanted to catch fish, drink the odd beer, and burp. Culture is such a subjective thing.

I knew that trouble loomed when I met him and the Widgeon at the landing. Sherman didn't exactly travel light, what with the library of field guides and the cello. The latter was left in the car after a

much-heated discussion. Then and there, Dr. Milqueboné received a
few pointers in the finer use of malediction.

Sherm then went on to tell me that he had read the "body of my
work," and he characterized it as being "abjectly scatological." I did-
n't understand his meaning but thanked him nonetheless. I'm always
polite to a fan.

We left the launch and began our float trip from hell. In three
days we were to arrive at the landing where Sherman's Volvo was
parked. I looked back to see the Widgeon snickering as his nephew
began a discourse on the conjugation of verbs, which was to continue well into the afternoon, made all the worse because the wobbly
pop sat forgotten on the tailgate.

You learn things about a fellow on a trip such as this—mostly
things you never really wanted to know, like Sherman's favorite opera,
for instance. It was *Carmine* by Bidet. And in three days, he was supposed sing the lead, using his falsetto voice, when he and the boys
from the Glee Club would unite in a stirring rendition. Nothing
would stop him from that pleasure, he vowed. God knows, I tried.

Not long into the trip, I was starting to think that I was paying a
lofty price for the privilege of tying streamers from someone's derelict
hairpiece. With his nose usually buried in his field guides and having
arms similar to those of his aunt, Sherman wasn't exactly a power-
house in the manual propulsion department. Still, I did catch the odd
bass or two as the river's current cradled us to our objective. Despite
forgetting the beer, I was in no hurry.

Sherman had quite a sense of humor, as evidenced by his antics
at the first portage. It was quite a belly flop down that waterfalls, and
his girl-like screaming was absolutely convincing, as was his ashen
face. He began to grow on me. All through the trip he kept cracking
me up like that.

Day three found us twenty miles shy of our destination. A situa-
tion that I found acceptable, even if young Milqueboné did not.
Terrified that he would miss his Glee Club assembly, he insisted that
I get him to the highway immediately. I pointed to the east, through

the cedar swamp. About a mile I guessed. With compass and hatchet in hand, he tore off before I could show him the well-groomed trail just down the ways. Now, here's where the story gets a little sketchy. . . .

Somewhere between the screeching of brakes and the shotgun blast, something definitely went wrong. Apparently, it was hellish in the swamp, what with the millions of mosquitoes, Sherman's allergies and all. Still, he hacked his way to the highway, parallel to the trail, just like a trooper.

A little knowledge can be a dangerous thing, and a prime example of this was when Sherman, whose arms and face were bloody from bug bites, decided to pack his face with mud, having read that this would deter the mossies. This came into play later, as you will see.

Even worse than a little knowledge is a little coincidence. Such as the one that occurred when Constable Lewis P. Hucks brand-new cruiser happened by just as Sherman emerged from the bush, arms bloody, hatchet waving, and face covered in swamp mud. Thank God for good brakes and soft bog.

Naturally, at a time like this, a man can't be faulted for having an overactive imagination. I mean, when a bloody, mud-covered, hatchet-wielding man comes running at your rapidly sinking car yelling, " I want your help!" in a falsetto voice through swollen lips, things are wide open for misinterpretation. The constable evidently heard, "I want your scalp!"

When put in that light, the shotgun blast was definitely in order. Fortunately, Hucks is a notoriously poor shot, and perhaps it was God's plan that he just shot the hatchet out of Sherman's hand. Could a wanna-be writer ask for a better and more gritty experience?

Later, we all had a good laugh at the station house. Everyone but Mildred and Dr. Milqueboné, who said his farewells amidst wild-eyed, nervous, and hurried packing. He never so much as left a tip. Mildred is still a little upset, too, having an undeveloped sense of humor and all. Regardless, if Mildred and Sherman still have an ax to grind, so be it. As for the Widgeon and me, well, we buried the hatchet soon after.

36

TALKING TO THE DUCKS

"QUACK! QUAAAACK! QUACK–QUACK–QUACK!" I BELTED out the seductive tones of a lovesick hen mallard while my slack-jawed wife looked on in utter astonishment. She seemed impressed with me, perhaps for the first time.

In my hand was a shiny new duck call, and I was smiling like a free-ranging chimp on a banana boat.

"How much did that thing cost, Bonzo?" she asked. The way she sputtered reminded me of an old outboard my uncle once owned. I basked in nostalgia.

Meanwhile, her nervous hands moved like a blur, and she motioned excitedly, very much like an extra in a bad Kung-Fu movie. She snatched the call violently and was soon marveling about the incredible deal that transformed my normally baritone voice into that of a lovelorn duck. I wouldn't have minded nearly so much if the lanyard hadn't been still attached to my neck.

"It's a thing of beauty, huh?" I croaked proudly, between shallow breaths.

"How much?" she repeated coldly. Her look was stern and some-how even scary. I made a mental note to pity my future son-in-law.

"You can use it in the off season," I said, not really meaning it.

"Answer the question, Daffy."

"Thirty bucks," I mumbled.

"Did I hear thirty?" she babbled like an excited auctioneer.

"Quack. Quack. Quaaackk!" I demonstrated once again, just so she'd fully appreciate the deal I got.

That did it. Impressed all to hell, she stormed off, incapable of formulating an audible response unless you include the muttered cursing. Once again, the wily mind of the hunter had triumphed.

Apparently, she was awestruck right up to dinner hour and even during, as I noticed while eating my self-prepared baloney sandwich. For some unfathomable reason, the thought of me spending thirty hard-earned dollars on an item that she described as "a glorified kazoo" irked her in a way that I had seldom accomplished before, even with my God-given talents for insensitivity and poor manners.

Like all great discoveries, this was accidental. The fact that my purchase coincided with our anniversary and essentially took place of the gift I forgot to buy might have added to her vexation. Perhaps, but a fellow would have to be a mind reader to be sure.

Later that evening, after a heart-to-heart chat, she and I agreed that it would be prudent for me to lock up the ammo and sleep with one eye open. Three days of groveling and a few dozen red roses were all it took before she softened enough to allow me to sleep on the couch. I considered this speedy reconciliation a breakthrough in our relationship. Within no time, we were back on speaking terms, but I was happy nonetheless. And why not? The blessed day had almost arrived and I possessed the call—my secret weapon—the one thing that would make me smarter than a duck. Which, in her considered opinion, was no small feat.

Opening morning found me down a channel in my favorite marsh, sitting in a newly erected cedar-covered blind, decoys set out, with my hunting buddy in the seat beside me. The rest of the boys were set up in two other blinds—one, two hundred yards up the channel, the other in a pothole on the far side of the trees. Together, we formed a duck's Bermuda Triangle with two hunters at each point. Six hunters. Six new duck calls. Six annoyed spouses. Six well-worn couches. A typical opening day.

As shooting light materialized, we put down our coffee cups, uncased our guns, and loaded up. Ducks traded back and forth in loose flocks. I snickered, knowing that with my new secret weapon they didn't stand a chance.

Mallards sounded off, and I nervously fondled the call. I remembered my wife's strange counsel with regard to using it: "Less is better." It occurred to me that this was the same advice she prescribed about my speaking my mind at social functions.

As this thought ripened, a trio of mallards circled our blind. Instinctively, I knew it was time to try out the call. My partner and I gave each other the nod. And then we spoke to the ducks. The problem was that we seemed to be telling them to go away. Which is what they did. They flew right across the trees into the pothole. Four quick shots echoed across the marsh.

Somewhat annoyed, we watched as two birds folded as neatly as a sergeant major's trousers during a short-arm inspection. The boys got them.

Not long after, a group of wood ducks flew between us and the guys up the creek. This time we took my wife's advice. The boys didn't. Instead, they called—pleading, whining, wanton cartoon duck noises. The woodies flew directly away from them and pitched in right over our decoys. We dropped two and thanked our pals.

The morning passed this way. Someone would spot ducks, call to them, and scare them to one of the other blinds. Because we were all in denial regarding our obvious lack of calling talent, we continued to provide each other with fine shooting. In the end, despite our calling, all of us did well.

When I arrived home, my adoring spouse was seated primly in the living room reading a women's magazine. I prayed that the issue didn't have one of those stupid surveys that are the bane of married men. It was too late to flee when I noticed she had a pencil in her hand.

"How'd you do?" she queried, as she cornered me under the kitchen sink.

"I got four mallards and a wood duck," I uttered nervously.

"Is that good?" she asked.

"It's like me putting my dirty laundry in the hamper all the time," said I, giving her a common point of reference.

"You had some sort of miracle happen?" she asked doubtfully.

I nodded.

"So your duck horn worked then?"

I gritted my teeth. There was the question that I feared.

"Oh yeah, my horn worked like a charm." I grimaced at the memory. "They must have thought I was a regular web-footed Louis Armstrong."

"Really? You actually talked to those poor, trusting ducks?" she asked incredulously.

It was the start of an interrogation. I had been married to the woman long enough to know that. Crafty as she was, she sensed my fear and knew I was holding back. I blame it all on the women's magazines. She looked at me in silence, waiting for a confession.

"All right, you win. The call was a god-awful failure. Every time I called at a duck, it flew away from me right to Dan. And Dan's call was no better. Every time he called a duck, it beelined out to me. Is that what you're wanting to hear?"

"Not at all." She smiled a cobralike smile.

I shuddered.

"But if that's the case, I have a simple solution to your problem, silly."

Sweet God up above, no! Not duck hunting advice, too! "What, pray tell, might that be?" I said, trying to remain calm.

"Call Dan and offer to trade calls. And after that there's this compatibility quiz. . . ."

37
NEVER CRY DUCK

MY BROTHER AND I STOOD BACK TO BACK WITH SHOTGUNS in hand, like two hillbilly line dancers. We waited patiently with our camouflaged heads sticking out of openings in the big cedar-covered blind into which we'd floated our boat before sunrise. Strange as it seems, neither of us felt or looked out of place.

This block of ornamental shrubbery stood alone in the middle of the wild rice beds, which, with us in it, was possibly the only talking cedar bush on that portion of the Trent River. Once a boatload of new fisherman with no concept of waterfowling or shotgun ranges, anchored twenty feet off our bow, thinking it provided what the fishing shows termed as "good structure." That old blind sure talked then, boy, and it used words that you wouldn't expect any clean-living cedar bush to know.

Admittedly, the blind stuck out like the Jolly Green Giant at a jockey club reunion, yet it generally provided us with fine open-water shooting. Mallards and wood ducks dropped their landing gear time and again to be with the attractive decoys set out in a J-formation, even though both my brother and I were quite sure that the birds were functionally illiterate.

In a setup like this, the ducks often appear when you are least expecting them. This has the same impact as, say, your wife dropping in at a stag party. You're only ready for this sort of thing if you see it coming, and even then it tends to frazzle your nerves. My brother, the bachelor, knew this.

"There's one," he hissed suddenly, causing me to spill my coffee.

Even though I was staring far off in the other direction, being an experienced waterfowler, I froze, and every scrawny muscle in my body tensed up like a garter snake caught in an electric pencil sharpener. Then, in those final few seconds before show time, my palms got sweaty, my heart raced, and my chest heaved just like in those romance novels that I have absolutely never bothered to read. I was a coiled spring, waiting for the word to turn and shoot over the decoys. But after about thirty seconds, Martin hadn't yet used his duck call. Instead of a feeding chuckle, he laughed the laugh of the congenital idiot. It was something he had down to a fine art.

I turned slowly to see him calmly sipping coffee and snickering.

"Don't do that!" I screamed.

It was the fifth time in the last hour that he had rattled my nerves with a false duck account. It didn't matter that I threatened to report him to Ducks Unlimited for fraudulent optimism above and beyond the call of duty. Apparently, that threat had no lasting impact. I was wondering if a gun butt to the head might be different.

"I won't do it any more," he said, smirking and crossing his rotten heart.

But I knew that like a hamster playing on a riverboat paddle, he couldn't quit if he tried. He was having too much fun at my expense, which has always been the cornerstone of our fraternal relationship. I did the only thing a self-respecting hunter could do in this sort of situation. I calmly threatened to empty my full bladder in, on, and around his new thermos. Unfortunately, this didn't phase him one bit, as he maintained that the difference probably wouldn't be noticeable

from the coffee I had brewed that morning. Foiled, I didn't know if I should feel insulted about my java-making prowess or complimented on the obviously fine quality of my bodily functions. Such is life for the egotistical.

In any case, within moments it happened again. I had just regained my composure, my heart had settled into a regular, reasonable beat, and my chest heaved only slightly (for effect), when he whispered once more, "Mallards off the bow!"

This time he began a series of urgent calls. But, of course, he wasn't going to fool me.

"You're a really bad actor, do you know that?" I snapped, just as the first boom of his autoloader interrupted. Two more quick shots followed.

My gun remained lower than a midget at a urinal, as I stood slack-jawed and watched the four remaining birds fly out. I looked at my brother and mumbled some sort of unpleasant suggestion that implicated our mother, all the while noting the two belly-up birds bobbing in the water. Needless to say, the ducks weren't the only ones a little miffed. Still, I take pride in my manners and so addressed him with the politeness required of gentlemen waterfowlers in the course of a hunt. "You stupid, silly, lying, #@%*!" I began. "We could have had them all."

"I said I'd stop faking you out, and I did," he answered through those god-awful pearly whites. "What more do you want?" All the while, he wore that I-just-got-some-and-you-didn't kind of smile that irks us sporting types.

"But you've never just told the truth like that before!" I yelled, pointing out the obvious.

"I've turned over a new leaf," he lied as he chuckled.

"You knew that would happen. It's just like that *Never Cry Wolf* story," I said, wondering if he had that classic in his picture book collection.

"It isn't like that book at all," he protested. "Ducks have feathers and quack."

"You better not do that again or I'll tell Mom," I whined. I knew that wasn't exactly mature, but it was the most potent incantation I knew of and one I hadn't resorted to in twenty years. Even so, although I was positive that it wouldn't work after all this time, it brought comfort nonetheless.

Martin, though, must have had some unresolved issues, because he went white, pouted, and nodded sullenly as I made a mental note to send Mom some flowers and candy.

"Let's just retrieve those birds and get on with it," I said in a very sullen tone.

Martin lowered and started the 9.5 horsepower outboard. I untied the aluminum boat from the blind.

"Ready," I said.

With that he nodded and began reversing us out of the blind.

"Duck," I stated nonchalantly while pointing behind him.

"Yeah, right," he smirked from his upright posture. Then, very abruptly, the last cross member of the blind's frame forcefully impeded the free rearward movement of his head. A hollow sounding thump echoed across the river as the boat now backed out of the blind unassisted. For a while there was no movement and only a barely audible whimpering. As he got up from the bottom of the craft, glasses askew, hat crooked, eyes still crossed, he looked at me with a very hurtful expression.

"I said 'duck.'"

And even though Martin might have seen stars in places where they never should have been, at that moment I knew that once again that all was right in the universe.

38

CONSERVATION AND THE THERMOS

DUCK HUNTING IS ONE OF MY FAVORITE EXCUSES TO BE surrounded by muskrats, cattails, sleet, and cold north winds. Then again, if you think about it, short of insanity there aren't very many other reasons that would be accepted in this day and age. This, of course, is truly regrettable, although the ducks might think otherwise.

If for no other reason than this, the modern duck hunter is a strange bird. He or she will think nothing of venturing into the marsh before the first warming rays of the sun, while normal types, such as fly fishers and grouse hunters, are still asleep, just dreaming of feathers.

Duck killing, the occasional spin-off of duck hunting, does happen during these forays, although not nearly as often as nonhunters and Disney cartoonists would have you believe. At least not while I have a full thermos, the overwhelming need for caffeine coursing through my weary veins, and a weak bladder. That's right, I'm a typical duck hunter. Or perhaps *waterfouler* is a better word?

As all duck hunters know, the thermos was invented by a duck sympathizer or, quite possibly, even a duck. The reason that I can assert this truth is simple. The fact is that a thermos and the taste-deficient coffee that all waterfowlers carry in it is without a doubt the greatest single aid to waterfowl conservation since the inception of Ducks Unlimited, falling leaves, yard work, and the rake combined. If you doubt this, go to any marsh and hold your scatter-gun at the ready. Nothing will happen. Now put down the weapon and pick up your thermos. Birds will appear out of nowhere and zip by singing praises to Juan Valdez while you spill scalding coffee on your lap and fumble for your gun. This will happen every time, and it is the primary reason that I wear a camouflaged bib, chest waders, and heat-retardant underwear during early-season hunts.

The sad fact is that we all know that this will happen on each and every expedition into the swamp, yet we continue to carry that demon thermos. I'd attribute this to an overdeveloped sense of fair play that we sportsmen have, but that isn't necessarily the case when my wits are pitted against those of an adolescent bluebill. Bluebills and others of their ilk are far more intelligent than their dull eyes tend to suggest. I, as any of my hunting buddies will attest, am not. Take, for example, the last encounter that I had with a diving duck.

Normally, as God is my witness, ducks tend to decoy to my elaborate spreads when I am in one of three thermos-induced modes: pouring coffee, drinking coffee, or dispensing coffee by-product onto the flora. Naturally, in every case but one I have my hands full, so it follows that the birds stand a fair chance of escaping any such encounter unharmed and with a better understanding of the hydrological cycle in general. This is the way I hunt, and believe me, you won't find this method in any manual on waterfowling.

But the bluebill I now write about didn't read any of those manuals, either. That crafty scaup decided to fluster me by flying in straight and level while I held my gun in hand. It was a textbook case of how it should occur. It's the kind of thing every waterfowler will tell you about, although never from personal experience.

Naturally, I didn't know what to do. And old habits, like fifty dollar bills and casinos, are hard to break. So, more by routine than need, I found myself automatically putting down my shotgun to zip up my fly before I prepared to shoot, as is the custom of every thermos-carrying waterfowler. The bird used this downtime to land amidst my decoys, and before my gun was reshouldered, pointed, and ready, it had taken cover behind Buford, my favorite decoy. Not that I would have shot that bird in the water. . . .

So there we were. The duck and all his wile against me and the twelve gauge. The odds were heavily in his favor. Nevertheless, I lined him up and yelled something like, "Fly! You son of a hen."

Did it move? Of course not. It just floated there doing ducklike things in the shadow of my favorite wooden block, knowing, as all ducks do, that I wouldn't put Buford in harm's way. I stood there patiently, gun at ready, and then I began hearing the faint sounds of Mother Nature's lecture on the diuretic effects of a full thermos of java. Or two. The duck, perhaps seeing my happy little dance and sensing that the dam was about to burst, tipped merrily and showed me its best side. This kind of effrontery from a diver was the duck-weed that broke the mallard's back.

"Fly!" I screamed through clenched teeth and yellowing eyes.

But the mooning bird did not. However, this primal scream did deter the flock of mallards who were apparently cupping in from behind me. As I looked at them, my gun at the ready, my jaw swaying in the breeze, the bluebill decided enough was enough and quietly skittered off. Just like that the excitement was over. Flustered, I put my gun down and reenacted the little teapot song for the benefit of the muskrats and cattails. The coffee, bad as it was, was only rented.

But while I struck this fountainlike pose, the mallards swung around and returned. Surprisingly, with my free hand, I reached for the twelve-bore and managed to knock down one drake despite the handicap. The remaining birds, having completed their intrusion on my privacy, left in startled amusement.

Look, I know it's not exactly a pretty picture. In fact, the only reason I tell of this encounter at all is to demonstrate the effect of the thermos on the hunt. And also to show that even with such disadvantages there is hope. Because, as demonstrated by this little story, even with a thermos nearby and birds in the sky, the average duck hunter can and will hold his own.

39

THE STREAMERS

LITTLE BOB AND I WERE AT THE CREEK ONCE AGAIN, ANGLING as we are apt to do in early springtime, when the water is dirty and high and there's no hope in hell. As futile as it seems, this sort of thing keeps a man away from the lawn mower and hedge trimmer, and is, consequently, in my opinion, good for the digestion. You wouldn't have known this, though, judging from the horrific noises emanating from my pal.

Our targets were trout, big steelhead fresh in from Lake Ontario. And though visible as flickering shades in the deep pool below, they were as cooperative as a hyperactive chimp with a chainsaw. These were not fishing show trout, that was for certain. They lacked that I'll-do-anything-to-be-on-TV drive that I look for in rainbow trout and talk show guests. Therefore, my buddy and I fished harder than was our custom—partly because we had promised our wives that there'd be fish for dinner, but mostly because of their reactions to that bold statement. After they stopped laughing long enough to compose themselves and realign wayward bra straps, they asked if reservations at the Red Lobster were in order. Little Bob and I shook our heads in denial, like two kindergarten boys who've just been busted with a handful of tacks. We then left, hoping to collect the ingredients for a home-cooked meal, one to be topped off by a silent slice of their seldom served humble pie.

With this weighing heavily on our minds, we drifted flies—dries, wets, and nymphs of every incarnation—past the upturned snouts of those unsympathetic steelhead. The most we would get for our efforts was a sarcastic wiggle of a tail fin and what I interpreted as an unimpressed sideways glance—the kind a man tends to get from his mother-in-law after showing off his latest attempts at home renovation. It was a type of look I was all too familiar with.

Little Bob, who was an acknowledged master of the obvious said, "They're just not biting." Several hours of intense field study had helped him arrive at that startling conclusion.

"We just haven't found the right lure yet," I replied, knowing full well that the right lure at this point would have probably been a fat, juicy, night crawler dangled below a red and white bobber attached to a seven-year-old via a three-foot rod and a Donald Duck reel. Steelhead can be warped like that, and to me, it's one of their most endearing qualities.

"There is no right fly today. Them fish are as hard to come by as teeth on a dang-blasted hen," said my buddy, who had watched one too many episodes of *Hee-Haw* during his formative years. The fact that he held a straw firmly between his teeth during the entire statement only confirmed this.

"We haven't tried plain old-fashioned streamers. Maybe they just want a mouthful," said I.

For lack of a better plan, Bob did a highly unusual thing. He agreed with me. "Let's do the streamer thing," he proclaimed in a confident way that said he'd take credit for the idea if it worked.

I soon realized that among the three hundred or so flies that I carried with me, there were no streamers. They were at home, in the special box, in the special place where I wouldn't forget them, although where that was escaped me at the time.

Fortunately, I had a portable, emergency fly-tying kit nearby in the trunk of my car. I believe the fact that it wasn't actually on my person does much to disprove the theory that I'm obsessed with that pastime. I suggested that we go back to the car, sit down, have a meal, and tie a couple of streamers for the late afternoon effort. Bob, being big, bearlike, and hungry, saw wisdom in this, once again proving that great minds think alike and fools seldom differ.

It wasn't long before we were at the car. Soon a sandwich filled the vast recesses of his gaping maw, and I unfurled the fly-tying kit in all its glory on the front seat and dashboard.

The big fellow looked at me and snorted cola out of his nostrils as I assembled all of the ingredients needed to tie my favorite streamer, the Black-Nosed Dace. Which was, coincidentally, what he looked like for that fleeting cola-spewing instant.

The real Dace, however, is a masterpiece of silver tinsel, black thread, red wool, and fur. The fur being layers of white and brown bucktail sandwiching a strip of black bear hair. It was a fly that had always served me well, unlike Little Bob who had never served me at all.

I smiled and reminisced about the trout that had fallen head over heels for this streamer like a drunk on a Stairmaster. It was a tried and true friend, if such can be said of flies. I ruminated on this while observing that the real flies thought the same of Little Bob, who had began snoring loudly while sprawled out in the shade of a nearby tree.

Yes, we would fish with Black-Nosed Daces or nothing. That simple streamer was the last desperate defense against the faithless wives and Red Lobsters of this world.

But just then I realized that I lacked the black bear hair to complete the list of magic ingredients required to bring the streamer to life. Suddenly, I understood the pain that Dr. Frankenstein must have felt before he located the ear bolts. And the thought was maddening.

Rummaging through my limited collection of dried-out road kills and pancaked plumage, I found nothing that could take the place of bear hair. And since we were not in bear country or even near a zoo, the possibilities looked dismal. All the while, my black-bearded companion slept, well, kind of like Gentle Ben. . . .

Later, after his nap and some frenzied tying on my part, we drifted, stripped, and retrieved Daces up and down the length of the creek. For all the stealth, effort, and sacrifice involved, the fish weren't much more cooperative.

But Little Bob felt the wind on his chin for the first time in years, and as last light faded from the creek bottom, he even stopped to smell the roses. Which, in this case, meant that he admired the pair of Daces I had provided him with.

"They are a nice and simple streamer, aren't they?" said he.

"Yes," I replied. "That they are."

"Is that bear hair between the bucktail?" he asked.

"A suitable substitute," I responded somewhat uneasily as he scratched his once-verdant chin and came to the bald-faced truth.

The rest of the story is not so pretty, especially my partner's glaring misuse of the English language and his libelous assertions about my mother. These were certainly not the kind of things a gentleman should say in the company of women while at a fine seafood restaurant. And I told him so, too—just before he attacked me with the lobster claw.

But that was a while back, and though it took nearly as long, the rift in our friendship, like the one in his beard, was all patched up eventually.

40

HARDMOUTHED AND BEYOND

As I write this, my feet know the pain earned from slogging through every grouse covert in the township. Wincing, I gingerly remove thorny twigs, pine pitch, burrs, thistles, and spruce needles from the uncharted depths of my soggy, half-frozen beard, while a wayward golden retriever sleeps contentedly at the base of my chair. Honey's nose is nuzzled dangerously inside my upturned boot, and it seems that the bad air she breathes only ferments further within her before quickly passing through with ample baritone accompaniment. It's not at all ladylike.

As I look around my den toward my shotgun that I've just cleaned, to the sporting books and back to the dog, I realize that this is the sort of scene you might see depicted in any sporting calendar. The smell of Hoppe's No. 9 hangs heavy in the air, still not totally drowned out by the smell of Honey's No. 10. Yet, despite the ambiance of it all, I am somehow troubled.

Minutes ago, my wife sensed this anguish and tried to cheer me up by suggesting that the dog had finally succumbed—not to exercise and a day afield, but rather to the toxic effects of my sweaty insoles. This would have been comforting had the children not overheard. Now all three of them are demanding that I perform CPR on a dog, whose exhaled air smells roughly the same at either end. Amidst their high-pitched wailing, I eject them from the premises and slam the door. The "Daddy Dearest" accusations hurt, yes, but they pale in comparison to the horrible secret that tears at this hunter's lonely heart.

If only the dog slept because of the toxic effects of my footwear. That, at least, would be a fitting end for a hunting partner who has until now traveled all of those miles as trusted company, the solitary eyewitness to entirely too many hunter–bird encounters, but who, to her credit, has had the decency to keep quiet about it all. No, reports of my dog's death are greatly exaggerated. She sleeps only because she is full. After all, two grouse—feathers, beaks, feet, and all—would satisfy the hunger of any midsized carnivore, don't you think?

Ashamed, I look at her, and she seems to be the very picture of loyalty and innocence. Suddenly, I realize that this is how my mother must have felt. Who knew that it would turn out this way for either of us? I can't help but think that maybe this is God's way of getting back at me for telling all those "the dog ate my homework" lies of my youth. Dad always said no good would come of it, and he constantly points to the fact that I am now an outdoor writer. But wrath of God or not, I must deal with it. This dog is not just a little hardmouthed, taking the odd tidbit of grouse meat. No, she is hardmouthed and beyond.

I had reason to suspect this earlier in the waterfowling season. While we were duck hunting, she and I were buzzed by a green-winged teal skimming the decoys at very first light. With the lightning fast reflexes of a veteran waterfowler, I swung at it hard and low. And as I opened my eyes, it was clear to me that I couldn't have missed. Yet, curiously, Honey returned only with a headless decoy.

Even then I was in denial. I said, "I must have not led it enough." As if this were possible. But this day in the coverts has removed all doubt in my mind. As hard as it is for me to lay blame, I must face the truth. It was never my shooting at all. It was the dog's ravenous appetite.

This morning, the first grouse rose from the base of an old, gnarled apple tree and took thundering flight through the hardwoods. Showing my characteristic flair for wing shooting, my gun came to shoulder via the inside of my suspenders. While busy untangling stock from midriff, I had no time to actually witness the imminent impact of shot and bird, but there was little doubt in my mind that mamma grouse would need to visit the singles bar real soon. After all, as I clipped my chin with the gun butt and bit my tongue, everything felt right.

The dog saw this, too, and ran to where the bird must have fallen. When a retriever does this, some people call it breaking. I call it anticipating a certain kill.

It took me awhile to climb that burr-covered slope, wool being what it is, but when I arrived at the scene, Honey merely stared sadly at me, then bit my gun several times. Following that strange display, she lay down whimpering with paws over her eyes in that mysterious way that hunting dogs seem to have. I'd give anything to know what she was trying to say.

A cursory search did not turn up the bird. We began circling the area, looking for the telltale puff of feathers, but to no avail. Suddenly, it struck me that the dog was only going through the motions and that her head hung imperceptibly lower like she was somehow ashamed. But no, it couldn't be. Honey had never eaten birds before. Or had she? I played the scene out in my mind: the flush, the suspender snapping back between my eyes, the frenzied shots and plaintive wail, and my satisfied gaze toward both skies where the blurred grouse had previously been. It was as obvious a kill as any grouse hunter could reasonably rationalize. Yet, not a feather or drop of blood sullied the snow. My gluttonous dog had left not a trace.

The second bird was no different from the first, provided that you substitute briars for suspenders and barbed wire for burrs. In either case, so complete was the dog's subterfuge that even the virgin snow,

where the birds must have dropped lifeless, was smoothed over so as to look entirely untouched by things plummeting from the sky and dog tracks.

Any inexperienced grouse hunter would have been fooled completely and laughed it off or blamed any number of things, none of which would have had anything to do with inept marksmanship or hardmouthed dogs. Yet, I saw through Honey's feigned enthusiasm, innocent eyes, and wagging tail. The sacred bond between hunter and dog was broken. Even as we entered the house she tried to act nonchalant—as if those two brilliant shots meant nothing.

Now, I sit here and ponder what to say to her. How do you explain grouse hunting etiquette to a delinquent golden retriever? Or that once trust is lost, there is nothing to share but cold sandwiches, cookies, and a dog brush? I look down at her peacefully sleeping form and suppress a manly tear. Frankly, I'm not sure what to do. I mean, it's that age-old grouse hunting question. Do I come clean with the truth or let a sleeping dog continue to lie for me?

41

FOOL HENS

WHEN RETURNING FROM A RUFFED GROUSE HUNT, IT'S NOT unusual for Honey and I to hang our heads lower than the tail end of a wet woodcock. Honey, in fact, will go one step further and actually smell like the tail end of a wet woodcock or something closely approximating that stench but on a far greater scale.

Maybe I ought to explain that my golden retriever, being a dog in good standing, believes that the primary purpose of a grouse hunting trip is to roll in every putrid mess found along the way. Her incredible nose is used solely to find these toxic piles and puddles. This, in my opinion, is the canine equivalent of using a God-given musical genius to play the kazoo. Of course, she won't put one paw into a thicket to bump a bird. Maybe it's because she doesn't quite get the meaning of getting all gamy. In any case, I don't like it, but I've come to accept this as part of the drill.

Despite the dog's failings, this is not always the way things turn out. Sometimes miracles do happen. Take, for instance, one fine autumn day last season when we discovered that just as there is a Jack for every Jill, there is also fool hen for every fool. The feathered proof was in my game pouch.

Look, I'll be the first to admit that referring to a ruffed grouse as a fool hen might seem disrespectful to those great game birds, and I certainly don't mean it that way. However, on that fateful day, we flushed five, and this was the only one that accepted a dinner invitation written in a rapidly approaching wall of No. 7 ½ shot. Einstein he was not. He flew straight at me, then veered off to intercept my pattern. For my part, it wasn't so much a good shot as a panicked case of self-defense. No jury in the land would have convicted me, despite the fact that my shooting is considered criminal in several jurisdictions.

On the morning that we left for that particular hunt, we never dreamed of such good fortune. All Honey and I ever expect is a walk through the coverts, a roll in fetid, long-dead things, and the sound of unseen wingbeats behind the next tree. Oh sure, sometimes there's the added bonus of getting impaled in the hawthorns while a grouse saunters off. But that's just my privilege. Honey never actually enters the thickets like I do. Instead, she'll wait in the open to cut off whatever flushes. But I've got to admit, when I sat back, removed thorns, and told her that she was just plain stupid, I never imagined that I'd have to eat my words.

Earlier that morning, as I donned my blaze orange vest and cap, my wife, Carol, reminded me that over the season we had somehow persuaded three birds to relocate to a colder climate—namely the freezer. One more, she said, was all that was needed for dinner.

"Know anyone who can shoot?" she asked smugly.

In the midst of this heartfelt disrespect, both the dog and I swore that we wouldn't come home empty-handed. We knew we must succeed or lie trying. It was a matter of hunter's pride. This time we would not let a bird known as fool hen outsmart those of the plainer variety.

That night when we returned to the house, Carol took an uncharacteristic interest in my presence. And, for once, I was happy about it.

"Get any?" she asked, fairly certain of the reply.

"I passed up on four," I said. "Too scrawny in the chest."

"Next you'll be telling me you didn't like their feather arrangements," she countered.

"Well, they weren't very photogenic. . . ."

She gave me her ritual look of disbelief. I assumed this grilling was in lieu of the one we should have had in the frying pan.

"I heard you shooting," she added. "Did you really miss every time?"

"I was thinning out birches," I replied. "Those poor birds almost collided with them. Lucky for them that I understand habitat improvement, you know. I expect some special award from the Ruffed Grouse Society."

"You're quite a conservationist. Does bird shot do a good job pruning trees?"

"Cheaper than a chainsaw," I reassured her.

Before we moved to the country, I harbored the silly illusion that being able to hunt on your own property might somehow be relaxing. Walking to nearby hunting grounds sounded good on paper, but unfortunately every shot was heard and required a thorough accounting to senior management. Good hunting tales come hard enough without being hemmed in by the limits of honesty. This time, however, things were different.

Suddenly, she noticed the brown lump hanging low inside my game pouch. "Did you run into a bear?" she asked hesitantly.

"No. Why?"

"Well . . . what's that at the seat of your pants?" she asked squeamishly.

"It's a partridge." I said.

"Will miracles never cease!" she screeched incredulously.

"Why so surprised? You think I can't hunt?"

"Well, no," she stumbled lamely. "It's just that you've got such a highly developed conservation ethic."

"Wanna know how I got it?" I asked.

She rose quickly and evacuated the room. Probably gone to get my pipe and smoking jacket, I surmised.

"Well, the underbrush was thick, too thick . . ." I began, looking off into the distance. A half-hour later, by which time I had reached the part about superb woodsmanship and instinct, she was still searching. It then occurred to me that I don't own a pipe or smoking jacket.

Honey and I went looking and soon found her huddled behind the couch. "Oh, there you are," I said. "Suddenly, Honey and I heard drumming over the ridge. . . ."

"Stop, please," she begged. "No more hunting stories!" Her eyes were wild. She held up knitting needles defiantly.

I was more dumbfounded than usual. Generally, she enjoyed my tales of daring-do. How else would you explain that frequent glazed-over look of excitement? "Is something wrong?" I asked, pretending to be sensitive.

"I don't want to hear how you got it," she answered.

"Sure you do," I corrected.

"No, not at all," she muttered sternly.

I walked away, dejected. What had happened to communication? Was this the end? If we didn't trade hunting stories, what else was there? Muttering among ourselves, Honey and I retired to my study.

Soon, Carol came in bearing a cup of tea. "I'm sorry," she said. "It's just that hunting is all you ever talk about. . . ."

"And?" I replied expectantly.

"Well, there's more to life. . . ."

Suddenly, it struck me. Of course, she was right. I looked to her and nodded. "How could I have been so blind after all these years?"

"Not blind," she assured me, "just insensitive."

"Yes, insensitive," I said, not really knowing what she meant. But a smile crossed my face, for it was time to make this right. "So, did I ever tell you about that big smallmouth I caught last year?" I asked, fairly certain that I was about to put this insensitive myth to rest.

But what happened next proved me wrong. As Carol flushed wildly from within the tangle of furniture, Honey, waiting in the open, did manage to cut her off. Despite Carol's screaming broad jump, no one was more surprised than me. Insensitive? Yeah, right. I apologized to my dog, didn't I?

42

KEEPERS

ON MOST DAYS, THE ODDS OF ME LANDING A KEEPER ARE about the same as the chances of a new crayon surviving a year of kindergarten—from slim to impossible. But sometimes miracles happen—crayons get rolled under the play center and cower there until year's end, for instance. Likewise, on occasion, I run into big, gullible fish, and that's when the real trouble begins.

I recently hooked a twenty-three inch lake trout on a short, ultralight spinning rod loaded with ridiculously thin, four-pound-test line. It was not a huge fish but certainly respectable for that central Ontario lake and the pint-sized tackle I was using. To be honest, it was an accident that happened while fishing for my traditional quarry: submerged logs, overhanging trees, water pump intake lines, impenetrable weed beds, and stunted panfish. Locally, I'm considered something of a legend when it comes to battling these things. Some will even tell you that I've never been skunked.

Anyhow, on that memorable day, I was in a canoe with my son, Ryan, who was six years old at the time. Now that's an age where a little knowledge is a dangerous thing, and just to prove it, he paddled us in tight circles, justifying this by arguing that the world was round, anyhow. The fact that I accepted this without further debate not only confirms that I am of unsound mind, but also has some bearing on the story.

"Why are you paddling us in circles, son?" I asked only once, as I switched rod hands and adjusted the reel's drag.

"We're men, Dad. Do we need a reason?" Ryan asked, somewhat perplexed.

"Well, yes . . . I suppose." I was going to tell him that it was a horrible waste of his energy, but little boys have no concept of an energy crisis. He could have done this all day. I needed something more logical. "Son, normally the fish circles the boat," I hinted. "It's rarely the other way around."

"I know," he said. "I bet that this oughta confuse that big old fish, huh, Dad?" he asked as I fought the feisty laker, spinning my head like an owl while changing rod hands repeatedly. I suppose it could have made it dizzy.

As if this predicament wasn't bad enough, the bugs were out in full force. Blackflies were attempting to carry us off and would have succeeded if not for the extra weight of those mosquitoes feeding on us. Fortunately, every now and then heavy gusts of wind provided relief. When combined with powerful currents, they also endeavored to make us one with the big cedar trees protruding from the jagged, rocky shoreline. It was the kind of day that made you glad to be alive. At least for the little time remaining. Trust me, these are the things you don't tell a boy's mother about.

It might sound strange, but I believe that the fish finally relented because it had a hard time fighting while laughing. It's my theory that this happens more often than fishery biologists and expert anglers would have us know, and it conveniently explains why clowns like me catch an inordinate number of the big fish. Bear in mind, however, that inordinate is a truly subjective term. In any case, there I was with a fistful of fins and mesh. The big laker was netted and my short ultra-

light rod was bent over at the double like a henpecked husband plant-
ing peas in the garden.

Even Ryan looked up and took notice. "Is that a big one,
Daddy?"

"Just average for an angler of my skill," I answered proudly.

"So what would a good fisherman get then?"

"Son," I replied flatly while boating the fish, "sometimes you bear
a startling resemblance to your mother."

Now, every article I've ever read on the subject of fishing will tell
how to catch, land, and release a lunker. But not one will advise on
what to do once it's in your canoe, bucking around like a hyperactive
Riverdancer. This, apparently, is something that anglers must figure
out for themselves.

The way I see it, first, there is the immediate problem of how to
dispatch the fish. Tradition dictates a gentle but loving tap to the top
of the skull with paddle—the kind my father used to demonstrate
regularly, often on fish, too. Though not exactly elegant, it is simple
and effective. But this is not easy to do while battling a self-made
whirlpool, bucking a headwind, and swatting flies. So, as my hard-
fought trophy tried to somersault over the starboard side, the shoreline approached faster than a June bug to a biker's teeth. Seeing this,
I steadied the fish and quickly administered the *coup de grâce*—that's
French for thunk!

Unfortunately, the fish's tail was centered between my knees and
directly below my Fruit of the Looms. And though it slipped my
mind, every school kid knows Newton's Law: for every action there is
an equal and opposite reaction. In this case, as the paddle dropped,
the tail rose just as quickly. And let's just say, not wanting to prove
Newton wrong, I reacted.

Ryan turned quickly, eager to see the nearby loon that he had just
heard wail. In the following minute of silence, we were carried into a
small sheltered cove, where I could mourn my losses in peace. For
once, I was grateful that it wasn't a bigger, more powerful fish.

"Fishing makes you happy, huh, Dad?" Ryan said philosophical-

ly, as I wore the strained smile of a baby filling a new set of diapers. I caught my breath, nodded my head, and slowly uncrossed my eyes.

I guess the stress of it all must have showed, because I hung my head in submission. It was time to cut my losses. "Home time," I muttered.

"Tired, Dad?"

"Bagged, son."

Enough said.

With dinner caught and a place cleared out in the tackle box for a jock strap, we paddled hard down the lake toward the landing. As the canoe glided in, we met another father and son angling team just beginning their day.

"Nice fish," the old man remarked.

"Thanks," said I, gingerly stepping ashore.

"I haven't caught one that size on this lake for a while. When I was about your age, I used to take my boy out, and we caught fish like that all the time. Hey, Billy, doesn't this remind you of a few years back?"

The teen-ager nodded solemnly, as if remembering a pleasant but long-faded encounter. As they launched their canoe, I saw him smile as he said, "Yeah, Dad, that fish sure rang a bell."

He didn't know how right he was. . . .

43
TRAINING DUMMIES

I STEPPED INSIDE THE HOUSE FEELING HAPPIER THAN A NESTING mallard watching a fox choke on a swan's wishbone. I've discovered that sometimes during the process of dog training, as in the sporting life itself, there are these fleeting moments of joy.

My wife momentarily stopped her knitting to look on suspiciously as she does whenever I exhibit out-and-out delight. It's not that she doesn't want me to be happy but more like she doesn't want to be seen as the cause of it. For some reason she equates my smiles with trouble, and the minute I flash teeth she tries to steer clear.

"Why the happy face?" she asked nervously.

"I got a new training dummy for the dog," I answered.

"What a shame—she was just getting used to you," she replied, then slunk off into the kitchen, away from ground zero. It occurred to me to ask where her winged monkeys and broom were, but I thought better of it. It's taken me years to understand, but there are some things better left unsaid just prior to hunting season. I shook my head and walked away. "Be careful of the water," I mumbled.

Actually, she's a fine woman, but her grasp on all things related to waterfowling is tenuous to say the least. Last year, when I told her that I had mistakenly shot a pair of shovelers in the bay behind the old cemetery, she just about fainted. Only afterward, when I explained that I was referring to ducks and not gravediggers, did she return to a shade that approximated her normal pallor.

In any case, this lack of waterfowling savvy was a major character flaw only redeemed by the fact that she consented to live with several of mine. Except for her mother and a few of her closest friends, most people called it a fair trade.

Still, I'll admit that buying a proper training dummy for Honey, our golden retriever, was her idea. Until that point, both the dog and I were content to use old socks filled with sand, which were all right for land retrieves but tough in deep water. That didn't bother me, though, for I figured Honey would be hell on diving ducks once she got the hang of it. And though this theory had merit, I relented and bought the floating dummy simply because my wife, like most women, couldn't abide wearing mismatched socks. It was a shame, too. Her feet are about the size of a mallard, and, although she doesn't know it, it was this fact that tipped the scales in favor of our marriage.

Despite our adventures with sand-filled socks, this dog training was new to me. Well, not totally. Long ago, I had a black Lab–mutt cross named Buck that I did train to retrieve birds. Usually someone else's, far across the bay, but still, the basic idea was there, and I must admit that with Buck around I saved money on shells.

Buck was the terror of the marsh and any other place that he escaped to. Like many hunting dogs, he had a terrible habit of rolling in dreadful, putrid, long-dead messes. Generally, he brought these in and laid them on my kitchen floor first. Buck was nothing if not domesticated. But enough about his good points.

In any case, years ago, Buck decided to leave me, and I imagine both of us have been happy ever since. Friends surmise that he has probably found a happy home at a sewage treatment facility in the big city, where he can swim in sludge, chase geese on the grass, and roll in the real good stuff all day long. For a while we entertained the possibility of his return, but our moving to the country changed all of that. Still, Buck's memory lingers on, and every time I hear see the movie *Swamp Thing* I think of him.

With Buck's ghost still haunting me, I was somewhat nervous about training Honey. It had been awhile since I had molded a dog in my image, and flashbacks of those long hours entangled in a hundred-foot check cord very nearly prevented this. Honey, however, showed promise. Not training her would have been a sin. Even as a young pup, she enthusiastically retrieved my slippers, and still does. Of course, the fact that I'm usually wearing them is a minor drawback, but it's comforting to know that she could drag a deer up and down a set of stairs if need be.

The major difference between her and Buck lies in the fact that Honey knows who the boss is. In spite of this, she'll take orders from me if my wife is not around. Nor is Honey spoiled like Buck was. She spends most of the time in her very own kennel and is more than content there. So, that day, I unkenneled her, gently rousing her from the couch. Fortunately, the movie was over, anyhow. It was time to get to the business of making a gun dog out of her. I looked into her eager eyes. She returned my bewildered gaze.

"Honey," I explained, "when I throw this dummy you will run over, pick it up, and retrieve it to my hand. There will be no messing around. You are a retriever and this is your lot in life." I always bet on the off chance that dogs and teen-agers understand English.

I lobbed the dummy high and out. Bang went the pistol. Whiz went the dog. Just like that. Fortunately, I had knee-high rubber boots on. It was not exactly the subject for a Rockwell painting. I surmised that we had a long road ahead before green heads would massage her gums.

I had her sit. The training dummy was hurled out, and the starter pistol was fired again, just like I used to do with the old sock. With outstretched arm, I commanded, "Fetch!"

There was a slight hesitation, then it happened. Springing forward like a wet towel in a locker room, focussed on the dummy like my father did during those adolescent lectures of my youth, it was marked and quickly picked up. Then, gently held in a soft mouth, carried straight back. No meandering, no stopping, eyes bright, head held high. You could see that she was proud as the dummy was dropped softly into my outstretched hand. We both knew it was a perfect retrieve.

"Now, you try it!" I said, spitting out what I hoped was merely sod.

Honey wagged her tail. She glanced at me with an understanding look frequently found in lower life forms and hunting buddies. And, with that faint hope, her formal education began.

As I said, it's been a while since I tried to train a dog, but like everything else about retrieving, I guess, eventually, it all comes back to you.

44
CARDINAL DIRECTIONS

THE YOUNG MAN WHO STUMBLED THROUGH THE THICKET TO confront me was wild-eyed, confused, terrified, and covered in cold sweat. However, at sixteen he hardly looked old enough to be married.

Intuitively, I understood that he had been hunting. His blaze orange parka and hat were subtle indicators. So, too, was the economy grade .410, which was unloaded and broken open across his shoulders. But now it seemed that he was hunting more for a way out of the woods than for the fool hens that had led him astray. In his trembling hands was an old Lensmatic compass. Of course, it would have been far more effective had he held it right side up.

"Lost?" I asked knowingly.

Sheepishly, he admitted as much.

I gave a comforting smile. From my position on the ridge top, I had listened to his progress all morning. Every now and then his little shotgun would sound off a tad closer than the time before, and I'd catch a glimpse of blaze orange tripping and tumbling through the thickets. By his advance, I could tell that he was headed straight for the middle of nowhere, a dangerous place filled with briars, hawthorns, blowdowns, and grapevines, a place where rookies often found themselves hopelessly lost and entangled. Coincidentally, I had been visiting that very place for the last two hours, just for old-time's sake. After he untangled me and pointed me back toward the trail, we began to chat in earnest about his dilemma.

"Have a seat and calm down," I urged, pacing tight circles and hyperventilating. "That's the first rule to follow once you realize you're lost. Of course, few outdoorsmen will admit that they are lost until they meet a nomadic tribe speaking an indecipherable language."

By his slack jaw and incoherent mumbling, I quickly ascertained that the boy was in shock. All of the signs were there. I mean, how many teen-aged boys would normally sit and listen this politely? Realizing that I had to act quickly, I commenced with the oldest outdoors ploy in the book. I searched the upper pocket of my hunting vest for a pipe. Naturally, I didn't have one, but it was a grand, outdoorsy gesture nevertheless. As a boy, I was quite impressed by absentminded old fools and their endless searches for errant pipes. There was something reassuring about this pastime that took your mind off important issues, like where in hell is the road?

"Have you lost something?" The young lad asked impatiently, no doubt sensing he was in the presence of a true outdoor genius. My ploy was obviously working.

"Uh . . . er . . . just my trusty old pipe. Carved it myself, out of antler, while the buck who wore it was sleeping," I boasted. I was hoping to instill additional confidence. In retrospect, I believe I might have gone overboard.

"Wait!" I yelled as he charged wildly through the nearest thicket.

"What for?" he answered. "You can't find your pipe, let alone the road!"

"Maybe so, but I have a map!"

He stopped cold, perhaps instinctively understanding the modern day topographical map's usefulness. The root he tripped over might have helped, too. Like all teens, a gazelle he was not.

I produced that old, well-used map and carefully unfolded it to get at the enclosed baloney sandwich. We both sat back and marveled at that technological advancement. After wolfing it down, we had a quick look at the map, too. As he studied it, his face seemed to glow. Later, I realized it was just mustard on his chin.

"When an outdoorsman opens up a map, several questions come to mind," I began authoritatively.

"Yeah," he mumbled dreamily. "What new lakes will this lead me to? Is that far-off ridge accessible? Does the monster buck of my fantasies live there?"

"Maybe," said I, smirking at his innocence. "But I was thinking of more practical things, like has my mother-in-law ever been there? Is it possible that she might return? And most importantly, how the hell to you fold these things up again?" The lad, enthusiastic as he was, had so much to learn.

"I guess I hadn't thought of folding it up again," he said timidly.

"Few outdoorsmen do," I asserted, turning it to what I guessed was right side up. "But map use, like so much else that we veteran outdoorsmen take for granted, is an art form."

"I suppose they've been around forever," said the young, directionally challenged nomad. "Probably since you were a kid."

"Earlier," I countered. "If memory serves me, and I can't recall if it ever did, the early Italians, specifically Marco Polo, were first to invent the topographical map. In fact, the origin of the expresssion *Topo Gigio,* means literally, 'lost rodent.' Which, coincidentally, is how Polo looked as he blundered into China. However, it wasn't until the minor Chinese refinements of the compass, cardinal directions, grid lines, contour lines, symbology, paper, and ink that the map was a truly useful navigational aid. Up until then, map-users generally went out on excursions and were never heard from again."

I paused for effect but mostly because I had lost my train of thought. The lad looked truly amazed by the wealth of geographical

knowledge that he had literally tripped over. Smoke was practically emanating from his youthful ears as he took it all in. Even I was impressed. It came back to me so clearly, skipped classes or not.

"What are you, some sort of cartographer?" he asked.

After reassuring him that I drove a pickup just like everyone else, I continued. "The basic theory behind map and compass use can be summarized by the simple expression, 'Wherever you go, there you are.' Bear this in mind as it will come in handy on most occasions."

"You've got to be kidding!" he replied incredulously, perhaps astonished by my simplicity, as, I'm told, most people are.

"Of course not," I answered. "If more outdoorsmen remembered this, the incidence of lost hunters would drop drastically. Conversely, there would be a rise in the number of hunters who could legitimately say, 'I wasn't lost. I was there, wherever the hell that was.'"

The boy was speechless, something I have only dreamed about with my own teen-ager, but I believe that he essentially grasped the tenuous concepts of map use. So I continued before his eye balls rolled back to their proper positions. "Once you've mastered that basic navigational tenet," I explained, "the rest is embarrassingly easy. There are two schools of thought on orienteering. The first being to get a map and compass, learn how to use them with unerring accuracy, and only get lost when you forget them at home."

"What's the second?" asked the now-curious teen. His head had started shaking from the weight of all this imparted knowledge.

"Always travel with a buddy who knows how to use these tools and has the memory of Jumbo," I replied, stating the obvious.

The kid, having sapped enough of my outdoor savvy, left quickly after that, his mind seemingly saturated. I smiled and felt good about passing off what I knew. And then I pulled out my Global Positioning System and made a beeline for home.

45

THE POOL SHARK

I
T'S OPENING DAY FOR STEELHEAD IN YOUR NECK OF THE WOODS. So you stalk a quiet pool on your favorite creek for a full quarter of an hour, crawling toward the edge of the bank like a geriatric tomcat with hemorrhoids. Turtles rush past you. Positioning yourself behind an overhanging tree, you quietly put on your polarized glasses and feel a strange urge to use a litter box. Instead, however, you settle on spraying a tree. With that taken care of, you get back to the business at hand and observe a pod of battle-hardened steelhead caught off guard—one of nature's finest sights.

The whites of their mouths are winking with each underwater morsel brought to them by the moderate current. You wink back. After all, it is the perfect setup. What could go wrong? Without any sudden movement, and that includes breathing, you produce a fly box full of soft-hackled wonders and began tying one on. As you are just about finished and ready for action, three Neanderthal-sized, opening-day wonders stomp down the same route, casting shadows and halitosis directly over the steelhead, which scatter like children at chore time.

These creek-bottom Sasquatches have apparently tied one on, too. If not today, then last night. Or maybe they're still working off last opener. At this point, it matters not—the pool is now emptier than a politician's promise. As you wipe a tear from your eye, they ask the magic question: "Any fish in that pool?"

Your options consist of: a) throwing them in for a closer look; b) inventing new and exciting lyrics for a gangsta rap tune; c) shaking your head and walking away because they are all definitely bigger than you and have dragging knuckles to boot.

Any of those answers are acceptable, as any serious stream fisherman will tell you, and answer b) might even buy you your own trout stream if it carries enough shock value and commercial success, but there is a better way. It's one I have spent many opening days developing, and it just might work for you, too.

The system, which for lack of a better name we'll call Steve's Marvelous and Repulsive Tactics at Stream Side (SMARTASS), consists of subtle clues and innuendoes designed to deter the unmannered worm-dunkers of opening day. I've found that nothing short of an irritated grizzly bear scooping up steelhead from a brush-choked creek is as effective in slowing up opening day fishermen. Maybe the SMARTASS system is even more effective. A lot of guys I've met would shoulder the bruin right out of the pool and not think twice. Then again, you should see some of their wives.

The system progresses from minor techniques to more extreme subterfuges, but beware. Even if all methods were used simultaneously, they wouldn't stop an angler who has witnessed you actually landing a fish. Once you've been caught in the act of successful fishing, you might as well move on over.

Still, there is hope for rescuing your solitude, as long as you see them coming first. Here's how to do it. . . .

1. At the first sign of a pool-thief tripping through the underbrush, flail a large weighted streamer through the air uncontrollably and scream, "Stand back! I'm new at

this!" For added effect, prior to starting, embed several flies deep in the trunks of the nearest hardwood trees, then spread shredded clothing and fake blood throughout the immediate area. A scarecrow impaled by a multitude of weighted streamers might be required on weekend openers.

2. If they have the bravery to penetrate this defense, begin primal scream therapy between disturbed mutterings about the undeservedness of that lengthy jail sentence. After all, you were just listening to the voices. Burn a pentagram on your forehead for that special added touch and talk lovingly about your mother-in-law.

3. The first two tactics alone probably won't be enough to deter anyone if there is a good fish in plain sight, however. It is at this point you that introduce yourself and begin a lengthy dissertation on your newly discovered feminine side. Giggle frequently and ask if your butt looks big in your new waders.

4. Add to this your views on the joys of male bonding (go right back to your earliest childhood recollections). Refer frequently to movies like *Spartacus* and the *Crying Game* as classics.

5. Use the wind to your advantage. Combine this with a whoopie cushion and some skunk cover scent, and keep asking for advice on anti-flatulents. (Be very careful here! You might open up a whole new can of worms, so to speak.) If waist-deep in water, use a live-well aerator to blow bubbles to the surface. All this, of course, can be ignored if you actually had Bean Surprise and beer the night before. If so, let nature take its course.

6. Talk about your many illnesses in great detail. If you run into a hypochondriac, you may have to resort to the vasectomy scar ploy. If he wants to compare, cut your losses and move on.

7. Invite prospective anglers to fish the spot. Then give a play-by-play commentary, pointing out every little flaw in their technique. A megaphone adds a lot to this ploy. Only do this if you think you can take them in a fair fight or outrun them to the parking lot.

8. Do stretching and warm-up exercises after each cast. Encourage them to do the same. A Richard Simmons-like voice helps here. Having Richard Simmons on hand is much better.

9. Begin a monotonously detailed dissertation on the aquatic insect life in the river. If you are like me and don't know enough about it to fill a thimble, simply make things up. Use Latin-sounding names, though—for example, *Ursus horribilis* nymph and *Cumulus nimbus* hatches. (Caution: if you run into an amateur entomologist, it may be you moving on.)

10. If all of these tactics fail, offer to share the pool, but all the while look upstream and speak sadly of the big one that just took Eduardo, your Chihuahua. Have a broken leash in your hand and a tear in your eye as you gaze off in the distance. A true steelheader will soon follow, feigning sympathy and offering condolences, all the while wearing a toothy grin and tying on a muskrat-sized fly.

That's all. As simple as they are, SMARTASS methods have kept me alone in some of the best pools in the finest rivers that Ontario has to offer. At least I think it's these methods.

Use my system and you may get that wide berth as well. But a warning: If I happen upon a muttering, flailing, leash-holding steelheader on an isolated section of creek, we just may share a pool, some fish, and perhaps even a primal scream or two. Hey, nothing is foolproof.

46

ROMANCE AND THE OUTDOORSMAN

RECENTLY, MY WIFE WAS READING ANOTHER ONE OF THOSE bodice-ripping paperbacks, the kind where the gaudy cover illustration depicts a muscular, bare-chested frontiersman embracing a buxom heroine clad only in a torn, sexy, low-cut gown.

Naturally, this caught my eye like a poorly cast streamer. And why not? It was an idyllic autumn scene, and they were lost in a passionate embrace. Unfortunately, this nonsense was happening in the middle of what appeared to be excellent grouse and woodcock habitat and right on a well-used deer trail that overlooked a blue ribbon trout stream. No doubt they were spooking all sorts of fish and game with their loud, messy lip smacking—after all, there's not a sound in nature that this sort of thing resembles more than the popping of a black bear's teeth. To make matters worse, the blinding whiteness and movement of her heaving and ample cleavage was sure to flag to every wise old buck in the valley. Besides, what kind of pinhead with long, flowing locks would be caught dead wearing frilly, red silk pantaloons in the middle of the untamed wilderness? Believe me, she was not a whole lot better prepared, either. To add further insult to injury, his musket, a .54 caliber customized Kentucky squirrel rifle with a beautifully checkered walnut stock and a one in forty-eight inch rifled twist, was propped carelessly against a tree. I also have good reason to suspect that he bent his gold-plated ramp blade, too.

Who the heck knows what this idiot was thinking? The fool was courting the woman when he could have impressed her even more by scaring up a squirrel or two for her to skin, clean, and cook. Hey, I might not be Fabio, but I know a thing or two about romance in the outdoors. The old squirrel ploy leaves them teary-eyed and speechless every time. Trust me. It worked without fail on my ex-wife.

After thinking about all this, I couldn't help but snicker aloud. Obviously, that book was written by a person with little or no experience in affairs of the heart. Oh, sure, that old spinster of an author probably knew a bit about romance, but what right did she have to sully an otherwise decent tale of upland game hunting? I say leave these matters of love to those of us who know them best.

Just then I caught glimpse of his Bowie knife. It was far to big for any practical camp use, sheathed in a buckskin case decorated with more oyster shell beads and colorful tassels than you'd see at Mardi Gras. Naturally, I broke out into a belly laugh, and spewed one stream of scalding coffee out of each nostril. No small trick with that cold, I might add.

Surprisingly, my wife noticed this subtlety and asked impatiently why I was simultaneously chortling and whimpering. Now bear in mind that she has never read one of my epics, so has no basis for reference when it comes to identifying fine literature. Perhaps it is for this reason that she has elevated these romance books to the category of Shakespeare's misspelled drivel and is quite defensive about them.

"What are you laughing at?" she repeated.

I quickly realized that it was for just such occasions that little white lies were created. As I was sifting through my depleted memory banks for one, it occurred to me that a big white lie probably wouldn't be overkill, either.

"It's those funny lines on his stomach. What are they?" I asked, steering clear of the oft-misunderstood I'd-rather-hunt-than-embrace-you-in-the-woods issue.

"They're called abdominal muscles. He has a washboard stomach," she said, slurring her words because she began to drool uncontrollably.

"Thinking of broiled squirrel?" I asked, always sensitive to her every nuance.

"What?" she replied, perhaps not realizing that I knew her better than she even knew herself.

"Uh, never mind. Tell me more about this washboard stomach," I said. "Like where, for instance, is the rest of it?"

"That's all there is," she confirmed dreamily.

"Are you sure?" I questioned suspiciously.

"Yes, he's the unknowing heir to a railway empire, a wrongly accused fugitive, an Apache warrior–prince, and a sensitive and caring poet who happens to have the taut, tanned, and glistening body of a Greek god. And his hobbies are cooking, foot massage and cleaning. . . ."

"Fiction, right?" I asserted.

"Historical fiction," she corrected, "but entirely plausible."

Now bear in mind that this is a woman who won't believe that I once had a full head of hair.

"Yeah, well, I can tell you he isn't an outdoorsman," I retorted.

"The stomach, huh?"

"Absolutely!"

It's not that outdoorsmen don't have washboard stomachs—we do. But mine is strictly for fine washables—actually, several at a time. Moreover, a couple of my hunting buddies also seem to have wash basin attachments that shelter their feet from the rain which, of course, is an important consideration when you are exposed to the elements. And believe me, these guys are exposed several times a day, depending on their fluid intake the night before. This just shows that, unlike romance novel heroes, outdoorsmen are practical. You won't

catch us wearing skintight buckskins and frilly silk shirts during deer season. Not without losing a really tough bet. No, in matters of fashion, an outdoorsman has an eye for the more subtle shades, like blaze orange or tree bark, depending on the season.

My wife laments that she is spoiled by my cougarlike physique and fashion sense. Not to brag, but once after I took my "Pull My

Finger!" tee shirt off at a public beach, she said I spoiled it for several other women in the vicinity, too. And believe me, I must have. She's not one to throw around compliments.

So what's my secret? First off, diet is important. Typically, before the season, I follow a strict diet based on the Canadian food guide. Usually I follow it with one or two desserts and a second helping of the main course. This gives me the energy needed to fall asleep on the deer stand. Otherwise, my grumbling stomach would alert the deer.

Exercise also plays a small part in my pre-season preparation—a very small part, I'm happy to say.

Once I tried a push-up and very nearly succeeded, having mastered the downward cycle almost immediately. However, fear of a repetitive motion injury prevented me from breaking the plural barrier. It's just as well. Hunters with biceps are the first ones asked to help drag moose out of the swamp. Conversely, I have never been asked to drag so much as a snipe.

The bottom line here is that you don't have to be able to run like a deer to be an outdoorsman. Then again, it sure helps when you return from a hunt, look at her lovingly, and lay that brace of squirrels down on the counter.

47

ROAD RASH

THE LOGGING ROAD AHEAD LOOKED LIKE A PLACE WHERE A herd of hippos might wallow if they only had the nerve. Beyond the immediate stretch of impassable mud, crankcase-high rocks, chest-deep ruts, fallen trees, and pools of water deep enough to hold lake trout—beyond all that—was uncharted territory, a place where a fellow might finally find a grouse to shoot at and miss.

We had hunted along the myriad of local trails for three days, driving to a likely spot, then wearing out boot leather like cheesecake at a bridal shower. But this exercise just gave everyone an excuse for seconds at dinner. It didn't produce a partridge. Any path that was easily accessed held few birds. Now, on the second-last day of our hunt, we were desperate. Not one of us relished the idea of going home skunked, especially since we had already done our bragging well in advance.

From the musty innards of the parked truck we took one final look at the obstacle that separated us from what we believed to be the happy hunting grounds. As he started the truck, Larry gazed off forlornly into the distance, smiled, and quietly said, "I figure we can cross this section if we just use high gear and take a crazy run at it." He patted the steering wheel of his subcompact, two-wheel-drive pickup. If you asked me, I had a better chance of securing a lifetime commitment from Pam Anderson.

"Is he nuts?" asked young Harold, the rookie hunter who accompanied us. He was generally sane and had never read about this sort of thing in the gentleman's grouse-hunting journals that he adored so much. Then again, Land Rover never made trucks like Larry's, either.

"Is he nuts?" I yelled looking Larry straight in the eye. "Of course he is! Forget high gear and fast—you need to put it low and go slow and steady."

Like Larry, I didn't have a clue about off-road driving, but I knew enough to offer a dissenting opinion on how to cross an impassable section of trail. Frankly, it's just about the best thing a passenger–sportsman can do—practically an ace in the hole. And believe me, hole is the operative word. When the truck finally does stall, as it inevitably will, this simple precaution allows a passenger–sportsman to assume the role of expert. These are the smart guys who direct the recovery of the floundering vehicle from high ground, all the while spouting out the obvious knowledge gained in hindsight, just like it was their idea in the first place. It's a simple survival strategy that saves back, legs, shoulders, and all of parts in between. Over the years, I've become a master of it. Strangely, this is something that outdoor scribes rarely write about, even though it's the kind of woods lore that can make or break a hunting experience, especially for new guys like Harold. Typically, while their shoulders are wedged between the bumper and a rock, and mud from the drive wheel plasters their innocent faces, they wonder why they didn't think of it first.

"Why don't we just park here and walk the remaining one hundred yards?" asked Harold naïvely, which, on the surface certainly would have been the intelligent thing to do. The young fellow was an original thinker, I'll give him that.

Larry was not in such a giving mood, though. In fact, it's a good thing I caught him as he lunged across the bench seat. It gave Harold the time to make it out the open window.

"Think I'm a girl, huh?" he growled as he followed hard on Harold's heels.

"Cool down, man!" I yelled. "The kid doesn't know any better."

It took awhile but, to Larry's credit, almost immediately after he treed the nimble young hunter, he calmed down somewhat.

Normally, I wouldn't abide such ignorant behavior, but you had to excuse Harold. He was relatively new to hunting and totally unaware that the sole purpose of a hunting truck is to carry several outdoorsmen and their gear deep into remote wilderness mud holes.

True hunting-truck drivers like Larry live for moments like these and, in fact, this is the best part of the sport for them. More than anyone, they understand that just getting stuck and, occasionally unstuck, can turn a good trip into a legendary one. For instance, no self-respecting hunter would ever say, "Remember that time when we were sensible enough to park the truck on the safe side of the old rope bridge?" They would, however, happily recount the time when they were jump-shooting puddle ducks from the truck as it got swept downstream. That's because the mere act of getting hopelessly mired justifies all of the shovels, picks, winches, sandbags, ropes, chains, boards, and jacks that have accumulated in the back of the truck since time began. It also guarantees future purchases. Just getting stuck and unstuck once gives a truck owner the moral high ground when arguing with his wife over the acquisition of a more powerful winch.

Before we go on, though, let's clarify that a hunting truck is more a state of mind than a vehicle type. I've known plenty of guys with four door family subcompacts who have managed, solely by willpower and imagination, to convert them into hunting trucks each September. The serious ones will even manage the progression of rust splotches so that a reasonable camouflage pattern emerges.

You know you are in the presence of a hunting truck purist when he looks down a rock-strewn goat path that edges a cliff and says something like, "You wouldn't believe the places where this truck has been."

Which is exactly what Larry said before he put his foot to the floor and quite possibly beyond. Just as promised, the truck charged forward—for about ten feet. With each rugged bounce, every low-slung part was jarred loose until I was certain that some were going to drop right off. Now, I'm no mechanic, but I imagine the same thing was happening to the truck, too.

Fortunately, it only took a few hours before we extricated ourselves with the help of Larry's new winch. Without it we might have never gathered enough wood to start the signal fire that summoned the fire crew and their heavy equipment.

48

YESTERDAY

THERE'S NOT AN OUTDOORSMAN ALIVE WHO HASN'T HEARD the phrase "You should have been here yesterday." These words are commonly used when the fish aren't biting or the ducks have settled in on the far side of the marsh.

It's also one of those key phrases that a fellow outdoorsman will use to bolster your misery on a day that already smells of skunk. Quite often it is the preamble before the story about the easy limit he got while standing right where you are now. Curiously, most often you'll hear it from some person you've never actually witnessed shoot or catch anything. That's because they'll tell you that they did it yesterday.

But all that doesn't matter. Whether the events actually happened is of no real consequence, because people will automatically believe the story anyway. This is because in any outdoor pursuit, and life in general for that matter, it's generally accepted that yesterday was far better than today. To me, the reason remains unclear. Let's face it, today often becomes yesterday within a day or so, and believe me, as I write this, I don't think that this particular day is any screaming hell. Yet, despite my misgivings, every sportsman I know will fondly reminisce about today long after it has come and gone. Whether it was spent fishing, hunting, or cleaning kennels, they will invariably describe the day in undeservedly glowing terms for no good reason at all, in much the same manner as they speak about their outdoors skills.

The truth is that I've never adhered to this philosophy. Maybe it's because almost all of my yesterdays could have been better if I just knew then what I think I know now. Such was the case a couple of days ago while launching a canoe on a small lake that purportedly holds big rainbow trout. Believe me, here is a prime example of a yesterday that could have been better. Much better.

Now, most outdoorsmen are aware that from space shuttles to kayak launches, one of the keys to success is to have a crew in the departing craft. NASA proved that even a chimp will suffice. It's a simple fact, and even though I was eating a banana, this thought slipped my mind. Soon, however, it struck me that this particular departure would have gone far more smoothly had I been in the boat. This kept running through my mind as the rebel craft strayed just out of reach like a yappy lap dog carrying a stolen hairpiece.

It was a borrowed canoe, so I wouldn't have cared nearly as much if my tackle boxes, wallet, car keys, lunch, fishing rods, trolling motor, depth finder, paddles, and camera equipment weren't slowly drifting off into the misty beyond. But they were. The only good part was that I was traveling light.

Much to my surprise, stomping, tree-thrashing, and loud, colorful, abusive language didn't turn the canoe around, as it might have in a perfect world. At best, all this bad karma just stalled it. There it hung, just out of reach, like your best dry fly caught in a tree during the biggest hatch of the year.

I sat and watched, hoping the breeze would nudge it my way. I even went so far as to create a little wind of my own. But, unimpressed, the boat remained in place as if it had been anchored at both ends, a trick I could never get it to do, even with two real anchors.

After a while, I decided that time for action was at hand. Looking around, I made sure no one was in sight, then undressed and stashed my clothes on an old stump. Naked as the day I was born, but considerably hairier, I eased into the water for a dreaded polar bear swim to the canoe. I did this secure in the knowledge that snapping turtles were still lethargic and that this wasn't a muskie lake. Even if it was, I was reasonably certain that the ensuing shrinkage would make anything resembling bait more elusive and perhaps less appealing.

I've never been a fast swimmer, but frigid May waters provided a competitive edge. I believe I was aquaplaning by the time my hand reached the canoe, and I was soon leading it back like a stray calf to the barn. So far, so good. Naturally, the mere ease of it all made me nervous, and rightly so. Just as I was ready to emerge from the icy water's frigid death grip, I heard voices—and not the usual ones either. This time they emanated from a group of female cottagers who were sauntering down the road toward the landing, picking wildflowers as they went. Ironically, my own petals were beginning to wilt.

Despite numbed extremities, I decided that discretion was the better part of valor. So with all parts great and small, I swam to the other side of my canoe and guided it a hundred yards away to a secluded and muddy cove, where a fellow could emerge proudly with his head held high and all else suitably low. It was hard work but far preferable to showing a bunch of ladies a blue moon or worse. Shivering and splattered in mud, I happily set foot on dry land as casually as if this sort of thing happened on every outing. It doesn't. Really.

Now, I'm not the kind that tends to worry about little details, but must admit to feeling a bit uneasy after realizing that I'd never seen any fertility statues done in blue. With chattering teeth and goose bumps the size of golf balls, I began moving through the underbrush from tree to tree. Disoriented, dirty, and with a mere hundred yards of unfamiliar territory between me and my clothes, I was taken back to those happy college days. Maybe that's why I didn't hear them coming.

Still, if you are going to run into anyone in times like these, I suppose it's best that they be nearsighted old ladies who have probably seen it all anyway. To my good fortune, they were picking fiddleheads and, therefore, never quite looked up.

The big one might have been an opera singer in her youth, because she let out a yell that made my hair stand on end. All over. I took off with my white tail clearing the ferns every now and again as I bounded toward the road. In hindsight, I'm hoping this new understanding of deer escape tactics will help this fall. As an aside, it's not hard to cover two football fields when you've got the right motivation, although that hawthorn patch caused some minor delays.

Once at the car, I didn't waste time getting fully dressed. I recovered my gear just in time to avoid the old women's panicked exodus from the woods. My spinning wheels kicked up stones halfway across the lake, and I sped away without ever having even wet a line. But,

you know, I wasn't even halfway home when even that day was relegated to my sorry collection of yesterdays.

The next day found me back at the landing, hoping things had blown over. But as I untied the canoe, a group of cottagers bearing binoculars and video cameras approached.

"What's up?" I asked, fidgeting nervously.

"We're looking for Sasquatch," replied the big woman in the pith helmet.

"Sasquatch? You've got to be kidding," I laughed.

"Laugh all you want," said one old spinster, "but I saw him yesterday, a hideous half-man, half-beast. You should have been here."

I looked her square in the eye, fondled my chest hair and growled, "No doubt."

About the Author

Whether neck-deep in a bog or hopelessly lost in the uplands, Steve Galea takes outdoorsmen to places where they've probably been but don't care to admit. A popular columnist for *Ontario Out of Doors* magazine and several newspapers, Galea's humor has also appeared in unwitting publications such as *Buckmaster's, Retriever Journal,* and *Today's Parent.*

The Ontario Community Newspaper Association's Columnist of the Year for 2000 and Humor Columnist of the Year for 2001, the bewildered Galea has also received accolades for humor at the 2002 Magazine Awards and in the Canadian Community Newspaper Association's Best National Editorial category in 2001.

Steve, his wife Carol, three anonymous kids, and a befuddled golden retriever live on a one hundred-acre farm near Tory Hill, Ontario, where fishing, hunting, and the great outdoors are just a stumble away.

About the Illustrator

Having never won anything, Tom Goldsmith still manages to eke out an existence by riding on Steve Galea's coattails. A huge fan of olives, Tom has dropped out or been rejected from some of North America's most prestigious art programs.

Tom's lifelong ambition to paint the Sistine Chapel was recently thwarted by overzealous security at the site, condemning him to cartoon work and hunting and fishing with social misfits such as Steve Galea.

Tom lives in Coldwater, Ontario, with his wife, two kids, and too many dogs. More of his work can be viewed at www.timberdoodles.com.